Other Works by Eric J. Wittenberg

Gettysburg's Forgotten Cavalry Actions (1998)
We Have It Damned Hard Out Here: The Civil War Letters of Sgt. Thomas W. Smith, Sixth Pennsylvania Cavalry (1999)
One of Custer's Wolverines: The Civil War Letters of Brevet Brigadier General James H. Kidd, 6th Michigan Cavalry (2000)
Under Custer's Command: The Civil War Journal of James Henry Avery (2000)
At Custer's Side: The Civil War Writings of James Harvey Kidd (2001)
Plenty of Blame to Go Around: Sheridan's Second Raid and the Battle of Trevilian Station (2001)
With Sheridan in the Final Campaign Against Lee (2002)
Little Phil: A Reassessment of the Civil War Leadership of Gen. Philip H. Sheridan (2002)
Protecting the Flank: The Fights for Brinkerhoff's Ridge and East Cavalry Field, Battle of Gettysburg, July 2–3, 1863 (2002)
The Union Cavalry Comes of Age: Hartwood Church to Brandy Station, 1863 (2003)
The Battle of Monroe's Crossroads and the Civil War's Final Campaign (2006)
Plenty of Blame to Go Around: Jeb Stuart's Controversial Ride to Gettysburg (with J. David Petruzzi, 2006)
Rush's Lancers: The Sixth Pennsylvania Cavalry in the Civil War (2007)
One Continuous Fight: The Retreat from Gettysburg and the Pursuit of Lee's Army of Northern Virginia, July 4–14, 1863 (with J. David Petruzzi and Michael F. Nugent, 2008)
Like a Meteor Blazing Brightly: The Short but Controversial Life of Colonel Ulric Dahlgren (2009)
The Battle of Brandy Station: North America's Largest Cavalry Battle (2010)

The Battle of White Sulphur Springs

Averell Fails to Secure West Virginia

Eric J. Wittenberg

The History Press

Published by The History Press
Charleston, SC 29403
www.historypress.net

Cover images: Portrait of Colonel George S. Patton. *Courtesy of Virginia Military Institute Archives*; Portrait of General William W. Averell. *Courtesy of Brady National Photographic Art Gallery*.

First published 2011

Manufactured in the United States

ISBN 978.1.60949.005.8

Library of Congress Cataloging-in-Publication Data

Wittenberg, Eric J., 1961-
The Battle of White Sulphur Springs : Averell fails to secure West Virginia / Eric J. Wittenberg.
p. cm.
Includes bibliographical references.
ISBN 978-1-60949-005-8
1. White Sulphur Springs, Battle of, White Sulphur Springs, W. Va., 1863. 2. West Virginia--History--Civil War, 1861-1865--Cavalry operations. 3. United States--History--Civil War, 1861-1865--Cavalry operations. 4. Averell, William Woods, 1832-1900. I. Title.
E475.7.W59 2011
973.7'35--dc23
2011036869

For Susan, with gratitude for her perpetual and cheerful willingness to serve as navigator, battlefield photographer and battlefield stomping companion.

Contents

Preface

In February 2010, my wife Susan and I were traveling west on I-64, headed for our home in Columbus, Ohio, after I spoke at a conference at Longwood University in Farmville, Virginia. We'd been on the road for a while and decided to stop. We got off I-64 at the White Sulphur Springs exit, which is the first westbound exit in West Virginia. After coming down the exit ramp and stopping at a convenience store there, I was stunned to find a West Virginia state historical marker that discussed the Battle of Dry Creek, fought on August 26–27, 1863. I eagerly read the marker and realized I had never heard of this battle, even though I had spent a fair amount of time studying the career and life of Brigadier General William Woods Averell, the Union commander in this engagement. I was intrigued, and I wanted to learn more about it. Later in the trip, we made a stop on the West Virginia Turnpike, and in the gift shop there, I found a book on Greenbrier County, West Virginia, in the Civil War and saw that it had a chapter on the battle, so I bought it.

When we got home, I eagerly tore into my new book, hoping to learn more about this mysterious battle that I had stumbled upon that day. The brief narrative of the battle contained in that book intrigued me further, so that night, I decided to tackle researching and writing about this battle because I realized that doing so was the only way I would really come to understand what happened there. The book you hold in your hands is the product of that research and writing.

I soon learned that the bulk of the battlefield was destroyed in the 1980s to build a strip shopping center. I also learned that there were three monuments just outside a fast-food restaurant that had been built on an out lot to the shopping center, so we made a point of visiting again a few weeks later when I returned to Virginia for another conference, this time at Liberty University in Lynchburg. I saw the monuments and became intrigued by the question of why there is a handsome granite monument with a bronze plaque to a German baron, Captain Paul von König, and decided to try to learn the baron's story. Researching him and his life proved to be a real challenge, and I hope that I have done his story justice.

A few notes are necessary to understand my interpretation of this battle. First, this engagement has at least five different names. Union veterans tended to call it the Battle of Rocky Gap. Confederate veterans usually referred to it as the Battle of Dry Creek, for the settlement located there. Others call it the Battle of Howard's Creek, and yet others call it the Battle of the Law Books. More modern treatments have called it the Battle of White Sulphur Springs, and I have elected to use the more modern name in this book. Hence, unless I am quoting from a source, all references to the battle will be to the Battle of White Sulphur Springs. However, the reader should understand that references to the Battle of Dry Creek or to the Battle of Rocky Gap in the primary source material all refer to the same engagement.

Second, the overwhelming majority of the soldiers who fought at White Sulphur Springs came from what we now know as the state of West Virginia. However, at the beginning of the Civil War, the area that constitutes West Virginia was still part of the commonwealth of Virginia. The state of West Virginia only came into being on June 20, 1863, and many residents of the new state remained loyal to the commonwealth and fought for the Confederacy. But many also fought for the Union, and most of the Federal regiments were only redesignated as being from West Virginia and not from Virginia at Bridgeport, West Virginia, on May 20, 1863. For many people, and especially for the Confederates, these units still carried a designation of being from Virginia in the summer of 1863. In order to avoid confusion, I refer to them as West Virginia units here. Further, the West Virginia regiments of Averell's Fourth Separate Brigade had just been converted from infantry to mounted infantry at the time of the battle, and they had not yet been redesignated as cavalry. They were redesignated as cavalry in 1864. I have elected to refer to them by their original designations—as infantry regiments—rather than by their subsequent mounted infantry and cavalry designations for the simple reason that the contemporary accounts of this campaign use the infantry designations, and it would be far more confusing to the reader to change them than to simply use their original designations.

Any errors of interpretation set forth herein are exclusively my own, and I take responsibility for them as such.

As with any project of this nature, I owe a number of debts of gratitude that may never be repaid. First and foremost, I am grateful to Terry Lowry, the dean of West Virginia Civil War Historians. Terry not only arranged a tour of the battlefield—all of which is private property—and escorted me on it, but he also provided me with the contents of the research files that he has spent years accumulating, greatly shortcutting my process of gathering material for this project. Finally, Terry reviewed this manuscript for me in order to identify and correct the inevitable factual errors that I made along the way. Steve Cunningham, the authority on the 7th West Virginia Cavalry, also provided me with some research material and many of the photographs of participants that grace these pages and reviewed the manuscript for me. Brian Stuart Kesterson, who had an ancestor who fought at White Sulphur Springs and is also an authority on West Virginia Civil War history, provided me with the benefit of his insight and lots of interesting photographs of artifacts recovered from the battlefield and also reviewed the manuscript for me.

My friends Daniel Mallock and J. David Petruzzi both read the manuscript for me in order to ensure that even someone without any working knowledge of the battle could understand what happened there, and I appreciate their contributions a great deal. Duane Siskey and Chris Van Blargen both rendered invaluable research assistance, and I appreciate their help. Steve Stanley, the best cartographer in the business, drew the excellent maps that grace this volume, and I appreciate his contribution.

I also want to give a special thank-you to two people who played an invaluable role in the completion of this project. Finding information about Baron Paul von König proved to be a real challenge. Finding information about his ancient ennobled family proved even more difficult and was further complicated by the fact that I do not speak or read German. Hence, the few sources available on the Internet were useless to me. The current Baron von König, whose name is Dominik, provided invaluable information about his family, and about Paul von König in particular, that has never been seen before by anyone outside the family. Dominik is the great-great-nephew of Paul von König. Dominik and his son Florian, who works at the United Nations in New York, have been consistently gracious and unfailingly helpful, and both went out of their way to help a stranger. I owe them both an enormous debt of gratitude. Without their assistance, the biographical sketch of Paul von König that makes up Appendix B of this book would not have been possible.

I am likewise grateful to the good people at The History Press. This is the second book we've done together, and I enjoy working with them. I am particularly grateful to Will McKay, who shepherded this project to completion. I had some medical issues that delayed this book for a number of months, and for the first time in my writing career, I did not deliver a manuscript on or before my deadline. Thanks to Will, what might have been a thoroughly unpleasant situation was made easy.

Finally, and as always, I owe the greatest debt of gratitude of all to my best friend, traveling companion, battlefield photographer and much-loved wife, Susan. Without her love and unwavering support, none of my historical work would be possible.

Introduction

The secession crisis of 1861 hit the Commonwealth of Virginia harder than most states. Virginia did not secede during the original wave of secessions after the election of President Abraham Lincoln, as the state's population was deeply divided on the question. It did not pass an ordinance of secession until after Lincoln called for volunteers to put down the rebellion following the surrender of Fort Sumter.

Not all Virginians supported secession. A referendum on secession was held on May 23, 1861. Twenty-five counties in the northwestern section of Virginia opposed secession and delivered majorities for the Union. A two-week-long convention met in Wheeling on June 11, 1861. The delegates represented thirty-eight counties, five of which were east of the Allegheny Mountains. The purpose of the convention was to discuss splitting northwestern Virginia from the rest of the commonwealth to form a new state that would remain loyal to the Union. The convention adopted an ordinance for reorganization of the state government on June 19 and then undertook the task of developing a government and infrastructure for the new state.[1]

In the fall of 1861, the voters of "Restored" Virginia approved the severing of thirty-nine counties from the rest of Virginia. The vote was nearly unanimous. The process of creating a new state began almost immediately. It took time to define the precise boundaries of the new state, and a constitution had to be drafted. The legislature of the "Restored

Government" of Virginia had to approve the severance of the new state, which occurred on May 13, 1862. The act included forty-eight counties of "the old Commonwealth."

Once the Restored Government's legislature approved the split, the United States Congress had to approve the admission of the new state to the Union. On May 29, 1862, Senator Waitman T. Willey, from Morgantown, submitted a petition for the admission of West Virginia in the U.S. Senate. The original version of the bill called for the addition of more counties to the new state and the gradual emancipation of slaves, but Senator Charles Sumner of Massachusetts offered an amendment requiring immediate emancipation. When that amendment failed, Willey offered a substitute amendment that called for the admission of West Virginia as a state as soon as the constitutional convention reconvened and accepted a proposal that all slave children born after July 4, 1863, would be freed.[2]

This amendment also failed, leading to more political wrangling over the question of the emancipation of the slaves. Fortunately, a compromise was finally reached. Known as the Willey Amendment for its sponsor, Senator Willey, it provided that all slaves under the age of twenty-one on July 4, 1863, would be freed upon reaching that age.[3] The Willey Amendment passed, and on July 14, 1862, the statehood bill was enacted.[4]

When the statehood legislation was brought to Lincoln for signature, the president was "distressed by its passage" and asked the members of his cabinet for written opinions regarding the constitutionality of the act, as well as the political expediency of admitting West Virginia to the Union. The six sitting cabinet officers split on the question, and Lincoln agonized over whether admitting a new state to the Union under the circumstances would be unconstitutional. He finally signed the bill on December 31, 1862, believing the admission of the thirty-fifth state to be "expedient."[5]

A condition of admitting West Virginia to the Union was the redrafting of the new state's constitution to include the emancipation provisions, which took time to convene and approve. The new constitution then had to be submitted for approval by the voters of the new state, who approved it. The results were certified to President Lincoln, who issued a proclamation that sixty days from the date of issue—April 20, 1863—West Virginia would become a state.[6]

The birth of the new state did not go smoothly. In the spring of 1863, determined to break up the critical supply line of the Baltimore & Ohio

Railroad, General Robert E. Lee authorized a raid by the cavalry brigades of Brigadier General William E. "Grumble" Jones and Brigadier General John D. Imboden, the stated purpose of which was the destruction of the B&O at certain critical points, the defeat of Union troops in the area and the gathering of supplies and manpower for the Confederate armies. The month-long raid penetrated deep into West Virginia but failed to prevent the birth of the new state.[7]

After electing statewide officials, West Virginia formally became the Union's thirty-fifth state on June 20, 1863. The new state lacked any infrastructure and, based on the commonwealth of Virginia's institutions and laws, created its own executive branch and cabinet offices, a bicameral legislature and its own judicial system, much of which had to be created from scratch.

West Virginia was a battleground right from the outset of the war. From the start, the Union controlled two of the four main transportation corridors through that portion of northwestern Virginia that became the state of West Virginia. The Federals controlled the Ohio River on the west and the Baltimore & Ohio Railroad on the north. The Confederates controlled the corridor to the east, beginning at a point between Winchester and Martinsburg to the north and Covington to the south. This critical corridor included the Virginia Central Railroad (connecting Richmond

The White Hotel, Greenbrier Resort, as it appeared in 1857. *West Virginia State Archives.*

and Covington, about twenty miles east of White Sulphur Springs) and the Virginia & Tennessee Railroad, which connected Richmond and Lynchburg to east Tennessee. The Kanawha and James River corridor was the central point of this grid, and it proved to be the most fought-over portion of the new state. The Union controlled the Kanawha River Valley, while the Confederates controlled the Greenbrier and Jackson River watersheds, with a mountainous no-man's land in between, leading to a protracted stalemate. Both sides tried to break this stalemate multiple times, with poor results for both.[8] West Virginia's loyalties remained divided for the duration of the war.

Greenbrier County rests in the southeastern portion of West Virginia, and its eastern county line also serves as the dividing line between Virginia and West Virginia. One of the world's most famous resorts, the Greenbrier, long known for the curative powers of its waters, is situated in the town of White Sulphur Springs, which is just a mile or two west of the state line. Greenbrier County held strong Confederate sympathies. It cast no votes for Abraham Lincoln in the 1860 election. It sent no delegates to

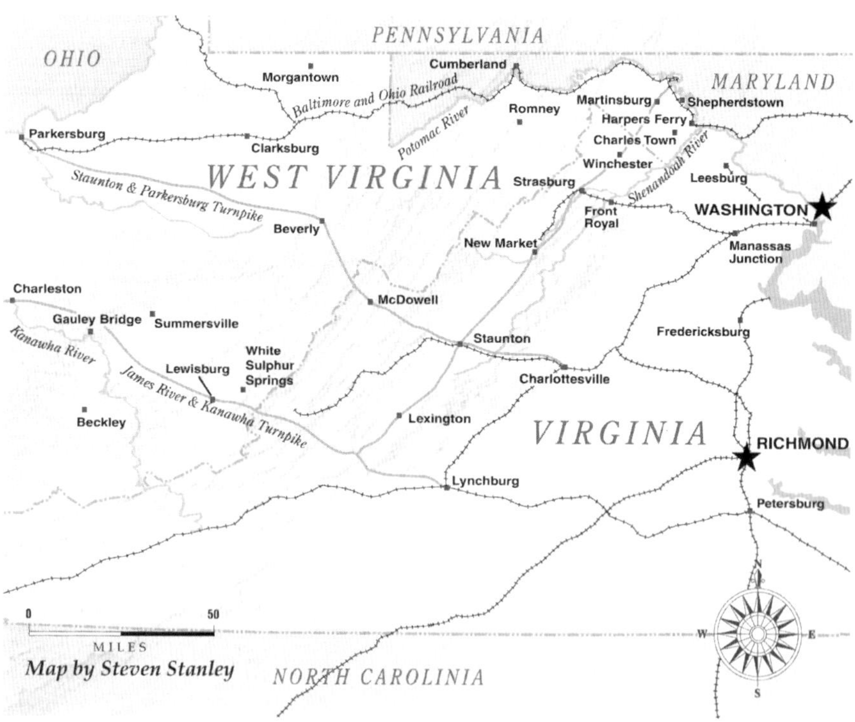

Theater of operations.

either Wheeling Convention. "Once the die [of secession] had been cast, Greenbrier County generally gave its loyalty to Virginia and the Confederacy as unreservedly as it had once extended its devotion to the Union," noted historian Otis K. Rice.[9]

The 1860 census indicated that there were 2,474 white male residents between the ages of eighteen and fifty-five residing in Greenbrier County. Of that number, about 2,000 served in the Confederate forces, while other men younger than eighteen and older than fifty-five from Greenbrier County enlisted in the Confederate service.[10] Greenbrier County had already served as a battleground more than once during the first two years of the Civil War. Union and Confederate forces clashed at Lewisburg, which was the county seat, in the spring of 1862, and the county changed hands several times during the early years of the conflict.[11]

Lewisburg is an old town and has served as the county seat since 1778.[12] While Greenbrier County was still a part of the commonwealth of Virginia, the state Supreme Court occasionally held sessions in Lewisburg, meaning that the court had to maintain a full law library at the county courthouse. The new government of West Virginia needed that full law library to help develop the judicial system for the nascent state.[13] Suddenly, quiet Lewisburg was about to become the eye of a gathering storm as Union and Confederate forces zeroed in on that law library. The hard hand of war was about to visit Greenbrier County again.

1

William Woods Averell and His Raiders

Brigadier General William Woods Averell was born in Cameron, New York, on November 5, 1832. He came from hardy stock—his father had been one of the first settlers of the area; his paternal grandfather, Ebenezer, was a Revolutionary War soldier; and his other great-grandfather, Solomon, was one of the early settlers of Connecticut.[14] His great-grandfather, Josiah Bartlett, was the first constitutional governor of New Hampshire and signed the Declaration of Independence.[15] Young William spent his youth in school and working as a drugstore clerk. He received an appointment to West Point in 1851, graduating in the bottom third of the class of 1855. Averell's superb skills as a horseman made him a natural for the cavalry. He was commissioned as a lieutenant in the Regiment of Mounted Rifles, later redesignated as the 3rd U.S. Cavalry. While at the military academy, Averell befriended cadet Fitzhugh Lee of Virginia, who was a nephew of the academy's superintendent, Lieutenant Colonel Robert E. Lee. Fitz Lee also wanted to serve in the cavalry, and the two grew as close as brothers, even though they were a year apart at the academy.[16]

Not long after being commissioned, Averell attended the Cavalry School at the Carlisle Barracks and spent a tour of duty as the adjutant to the commanding officer. In 1857, he transferred to a post in New Mexico, where he fought Indians and received a serious leg wound that nearly forced him to leave the service. He spent nearly two years hobbling around on crutches while on recuperative leave. Averell went to Washington with the coming of

Brigadier General William Woods Averell, commander of the Fourth Separate Brigade, in a previously unpublished image taken when he was colonel of the 3rd Pennsylvania Cavalry. *Brian Stuart Kesterson.*

war in April 1861, seeking to return to duty. After a stint as a staff officer that placed him on the battlefield at First Bull Run in July 1861, Averell became colonel of the 3rd Pennsylvania Cavalry.

Although an ambitious man, Averell was a conservative commander. He believed that troops needed constant training and did not want to take them into the field if he did not believe them to be ready. As a result of his efforts, the 3rd Pennsylvania soon gained the reputation of being one of the best-trained and best-disciplined volunteer cavalry regiments assigned to the Army of the Potomac. "He was an excellent drillmaster, with proper views of what constituted proper discipline," recalled an admiring trooper. "Instruction in a systematic manner, with a view of preparing these men for the service expected of them, was commenced and persistently followed in the most industrious and painstaking manner."[17]

Under McClellan's leadership, Averell commanded a brigade of cavalry during the 1862 Peninsula Campaign, taking part in the operations at Yorktown, Williamsburg, Fair Oaks and Malvern Hill, and routed the Rebel cavalry in a skirmish at Sycamore Church on August 2, 1862. He fell victim to the so-called Chickahominy fever, a nasty and persistent malarial fever, in the aftermath of the Peninsula Campaign, requiring five weeks of recuperation. A relapse of the fever forced him to miss the Second Bull Run and Antietam Campaigns in the summer of 1862. When he returned to duty, he was promoted to brigadier general and assumed command of a division later that fall.[18] When the Army of the Potomac finally crossed the

Potomac River into the Loudoun Valley of Virginia, his division engaged in frequent skirmishing and, when the army advanced, was hotly engaged along the passes of the Blue Ridge.[19]

Averell's personality mirrored that of the army's commander, Major General George B. McClellan, a trait that cost him dearly. "McClellan and Averell would take time to reorganize, reequip and retrain their forces even if it meant stopping the momentum of battle. Lack of a visceral desire to aim for the jugular of a defeated enemy eventually would cost both men their commands," observed a modern historian.[20] Like McClellan, Averell was a Democrat. Averell did not trust politicians, and he certainly did not trust the Republican administration, whose bungling he blamed for the war. He also did not believe that amateur soldiers and politicians had any role in the army, believing that only professional soldiers like him should command large bodies of troops in the field. His haughtiness greatly hindered his military career in the highly politicized environment of the Army of the Potomac.

At the end of December 1862, Averell, who now commanded the cavalry brigade assigned to the Army of the Potomac's Center Grand Division, proposed a daring cavalry raid on Richmond. Averell wanted fifteen hundred of the Army of the Potomac's best mounted elements to demonstrate along the upper Rappahannock River while Averell led an expedition of one thousand picked men from a variety of units, including the U.S. Regular cavalry regiments. He wanted to cross the Rappahannock River at Kelly's Ford, advance to the Rapidan, cross it at Raccoon Ford and then cross the upper James River. He expected to destroy the railroads, bridges and telegraph lines between the Army of the Potomac's position and Richmond and intended to live off the land during his raid.[21] Averell wanted to dash to the crucial railroad junction at Petersburg and then on to Suffolk, disrupting lines of communication and supply in the Confederate rear. In the meantime, while Averell's horsemen wreaked havoc in the Southern rear, Major General Ambrose E. Burnside, now the commander of the Army of the Potomac, would take the main body, cross the river and either sever Lee's lines of supply or defeat him in battle. Averell proposed the North's first large-scale cavalry raid of the Civil War.

Burnside enthusiastically approved the plan and instructed Averell to make the necessary preparations. However, Confederate cavalry chief Major General J.E.B. Stuart had already set out on a raid of his own, the Christmas 1862 raid on Dumfries, near the army's rear. President Lincoln told Burnside to call off Averell's raid, stating, "I have good reason for saying you must not make a general movement of the army without letting me know." Lincoln probably scotched the planned raid in order to make certain that adequate mounted forces remained to chase after Stuart.[22] However, Averell had devised a bold and dashing plan that planted the seed for future raids on Richmond by the Union cavalry. Stuart's Christmas raid cost the Union cavalry the initiative, and instead of a glowing triumph, the Federal army faced another embarrassment at the hands of its plumed rival, Stuart.[23] However, Averell's audacious plan marked an important first for the mounted forces assigned to the Army of the Potomac. Averell's proposal would have taken an aggressive stance, which was not something that the Union cavalry had done to date. It also marked the beginning of a long-term dream of the Federal cavalry, the idea of a large-scale cavalry raid on the Confederate capital. Raiding not only became Averell's specialty, he also had more success at it than any other Union general during the Civil War.

During the long winter of the Army of the Potomac's discontent in 1862–63, rumors swirled. First, Burnside suffered a severe and bloody defeat at the December 13–14 Battle of Fredericksburg. Burnside then conceived of a follow-up campaign in January that bogged down in the deep, thick Virginia mud when torrential rains turned the roads impassable. At the end of January, Burnside was relieved of command at his own request after the misery of his failed Mud March, as it became known. Major General Joseph Hooker then assumed command of the Army of the Potomac.

"It is reported here that you will be made new chief of cavalry in this army," wrote a fellow officer to Averell on February 3. "I hope it is so if you would prefer it. The brigade cannot spare you because it does not know when it can get a commander."[24] Another rumor held that the Army of the Potomac would be broken up and its horse soldiers sent to South Carolina. A few days later, Averell received a letter from his old friend Captain William Redwood Price stating, "General [William S.] Rosecrans's [Army of the Cumberland] is greatly in need of Cavalry. I thought it might be of interest to you under existing circumstances. If the Army of the Potomac is to be divided up, you might feel inclined to make efforts to come to the Western Army."[25]

These were just rumors. Instead, Hooker massed the Army of the Potomac's cavalry into a single corps and placed Major General George Stoneman in command of it. Averell assumed command of the Second Cavalry Division, which included his own 3rd Pennsylvania Cavalry. His command bore the brunt of the winter fighting, first at Hartwood Church in February 1863 and then during the daylong Battle of Kelly's Ford, fought on St. Patrick's Day, March 17, 1863. Averell's troopers fought Stuart's vaunted horsemen—led by his old friend Fitz Lee—to a draw at Kelly's Ford and then withdrew, proving for the first time that the Union cavalry could go boot-to-boot with the best that J.E.B. Stuart's cavaliers had to offer.[26] "For gallant and meritorious services" at Kelly's Ford, Averell, whose regular army rank was still captain, received a brevet to major.

Hooker planned a massive movement of the Army of the Potomac that spring. He contemplated stealing a march around Lee's flank upriver from Fredericksburg, flanking the Army of Northern Virginia out of its strong positions at Fredericksburg and then interdicting Lee's lines of communication and supply with Richmond. Lee would then have to come out and fight the Army of the Potomac on ground of Hooker's choosing. As part of that plan, Hooker intended to send Stoneman's entire twelve-thousand-man Cavalry Corps on an interdiction raid deep into Virginia, but heavy rains delayed the commencement of the raid for nearly two weeks.

By then, the element of surprise had been lost, and when Stoneman finally moved two weeks later, the mission had changed. Averell's division only advanced a few miles beyond the Rappahannock River before running into stiff resistance from cavalry under the command of Brigadier General W.H.F. Lee. Repulsed, Averell fell back to Ely's Ford on the Rapidan River, not far from the main Union battle lines at Chancellorsville.

A livid Hooker relieved Averell of command on May 4, sending Brigadier General Alfred Pleasonton to deliver the bad news in person. Hooker claimed that Averell had entirely disregarded his orders for the expedition,

> *in consequence thereof, the services of nearly 4,000 cavalry were lost, or nearly lost, to the country during an eventful period, when it was his plain duty to have rendered services of incalculable value. It is not excuse or justification of his course that he received instructions from General Stoneman in conflict with my own, and it was his duty to know that neither of them afforded an excuse for his culpable indifference and inactivity. If he disregarded all instructions, it was his duty to do something. If the enemy did not come to him, he should have gone to the enemy.*

Hooker noted that Averell's command greatly outnumbered any enemy forces in the area, that his march was largely unopposed and that Averell's division covered more than fifty miles without fighting the enemy's cavalry. Hooker's greatest complaint, however, was:

> *It is unnecessary for me to add that this army will never be able to accomplish its mission under commanders who not only disregard their instructions, but at the same time display so little zeal and devotion in the performance of their duties. I could excuse General Averell in his disobedience if I could anywhere discover in his operations a desire to find and engage the enemy.*[27]

Twelve years after the war, Hooker remained bitter about Averell's conduct during the Stoneman Raid. "If he had attempted to give my orders a flagrant and full disobedience, he could not have made his dispositions to accomplish that purpose more complete," he complained in a letter to historian Samuel P. Bates. "He did not strike the Rail Road on the 3rd and encountered a train filled with prisoners and wounded men, but doing the Rail Road no damage, beyond a temporary delay…On the 3rd of May, hearing that Genl. Averell was not one day's march from me, I ordered him in, his loss having been two men wounded and one killed."[28]

Colonel William E. Doster of the 4th Pennsylvania Cavalry spotted Averell sitting alone in his headquarters tent on the day before the disconsolate general departed for Washington. Averell sat "quite alone," Doster observed, "with his head resting on his hand…dejected." Doster thought that the deposed division commander resembled "a condemned cavalry horse."[29]

When he arrived at Culpeper on May 1, Averell did just as Hooker ordered, directing his attentions to the Confederate railroads. He chased off the Southern defenders and obeyed the orders of his direct superior, Stoneman, who had instructed Averell to push the Confederates to Rapidan Station and keep them fully occupied. Again, Averell did just as was instructed. He obeyed both the letter and the spirit of his orders. If Hooker had not recalled him, Averell would have reached Gordonsville by dark on May 2, but he never got the chance. Stoneman, Averell's direct superior, had given the division commander differing orders from those given by Hooker. Averell did what good soldiers do—he obeyed the orders of his direct superior. Averell realized that if he took care of his troopers, they would take care of their mission. His instinct to protect his command is often misconstrued as undue caution and lack of aggressiveness. The New Yorker was keenly aware of his duty to protect the lives of the soldiers entrusted to his command, and he always acted accordingly. Undoubtedly, Hooker's inability to communicate with Averell further aggravated the situation.

In his zeal to find scapegoats for the disaster that befell him at Chancellorsville, Hooker directed his wrath at the unfortunate Averell. When he reported to the adjutant general of the army in Washington, D.C., Averell did not go quietly: "[A]s the orders seem to be unjust towards him, he asks for an enquiry respecting his conduct."[30] His request for a court of inquiry was swept under the rug, and nothing more came of it.

On May 14, Averell noted in his diary, "Tried to gain some satisfaction at War Dept. did not succeed." A few days later, he recorded, "[C]ould get no explanation of the causes of my being relieved from my command in the Army of the Potomac."[31] Averell knew that Hooker intended to scapegoat him for the loss at Chancellorsville, and he resisted it to the best of his ability, ensuring that the official records reflected his protest and declarations of innocence.[32] The experience crushed Averell, who never forgave Hooker for the treatment he received at the commanding general's hands.

However, William Averell was nothing if not a good soldier, so he obeyed the orders, boarded a train of the Baltimore & Ohio Railroad and reported to Wheeling, where, on May 23, he assumed command of the Fourth Separate Brigade, a ragtag command of cavalry and infantry from Ohio, Pennsylvania and West Virginia. These undisciplined troops desperately needed a firm hand and training, and Averell was just the man to turn them into a reliable command. The success of the Jones-Imboden Raid had caused the Federal high command to reevaluate its strategy for fending off cavalry raids. Small outposts of infantry were scattered throughout the mountains, but without much cavalry support, meaning that the Union units were not very mobile and not able to react quickly to cavalry raids. The ineffective response to the advance of Jones's cavalry as far north as Morgantown brought about a change in strategy, and Averell was just the man to make it happen.[33]

"General Averell and staff arrived here yesterday afternoon and today after Church we had a grand parade and review of all the force here," noted one of Averell's new soldiers. "Infantry, Cavalry, and Artillery all together—it was a nice show, but it was awful warm."[34] The men of the Fourth Independent Brigade saluted Averell's assumption of command "with demonstrations of genuine rejoicing by the officers and men," as one veteran recalled.[35] His new command took an instant liking to the New Yorker. One of his West Virginians recalled that they "always had a great liking for the dashing general and admired his courage and ability" and also observed that Averell "was one of the ablest cavalry officers in the army."[36] Another noted, "General Averell's reputation as a gallant and successful cavalry fighter had preceded his coming by several months, and to be placed under such a leader was inspiring to these troops, who were at all times eager for the active operations of war."[37] With good leadership, the Fourth Separate Brigade could become a good, reliable command.

The Fourth Separate Brigade consisted of three regiments of West Virginia infantry, the 14th Pennsylvania Cavalry, Major Thomas Gibson's Independent Cavalry Battalion, Battery G of the 1st West Virginia Light Artillery and a signal detachment of the 68th New York Infantry.[38] His brigade probably numbered about sixteen to eighteen hundred men at the time that he took command on May 23.[39]

Averell immediately converted the 2nd, 3rd and 8th West Virginia Infantry Regiments into mounted infantry and sent them to a "camp of instruction" near Clarksburg, where they received horses and cavalry accoutrements. The idea was to organize a highly mobile strike force that would be able to meet Confederate partisan rangers on their own ground, as the soldiers of the Fourth Separate Brigade were intimately familiar with the area and with the difficulties associated with mountain fighting. Unless they were mounted, the infantrymen would be unable to keep up with the enemy's cavalry. The Union high command specifically selected these regiments for this difficult and dangerous service.[40]

"We are to be made into a Cavalry Regiment and will have our horses in a few days," noted a soldier of the 8th West Virginia, "but as it will take some time to drill and break the horses in we will fall back to the [Baltimore & Ohio] rail road or somewhere near to prepare for active service. And when we are sufficiently drilled I have no doubt we will have active service to do. I believe it is the intention to make Cavalry of all the [West] Virginia troops as soon as horses can be had."[41]

The 3rd and 8th West Virginia were converted from infantry to mounted infantry "in…forty-eight hours by mounting the men on green horses."[42] Unfortunately, the new horse soldiers were stuck with poor mounts. "Horses were not shod, and horses cannot travel over the rugged roads of this country without shoes, without breaking down very soon," as Averell correctly

Colonel George R. Latham, commander of the 2nd West Virginia Mounted Infantry. *Ronnie Tront.*

observed.[43] However, given the strategic circumstances—a large-scale Confederate invasion of Pennsylvania that was already underway—these nags would have to do, and the newly mounted infantrymen would have to make do with a minimum of training.

Colonel George R. Latham commanded the 2nd West Virginia Mounted Infantry (later redesignated as the 5th West Virginia Cavalry). Latham was born near Haymarket, Virginia, on March 9, 1832. He attended local public schools as a child and then studied law. He was admitted to the Virginia bar in 1859, opening a practice in Grafton. Latham served as a delegate for the formation of West Virginia to the Wheeling Convention of 1861. A staunch Unionist, and in defiance of active Confederate recruitment then going on in Grafton, Latham nailed an American flag over his door and began enlisting troops for the Federal cause. By May 15, 1861, Latham had enrolled a full company and was using the streets of Grafton as a drill ground. On May 21, he was called to Wheeling to arrange to have his "Grafton Guards" mustered into service and was commissioned captain of Company B, 2nd

West Virginia Infantry. He then was promoted to colonel of the regiment on May 24, 1862.[44]

The 2nd West Virginia was the first West Virginia regiment enlisted for three years' service and was also the first mustered in under Governor Francis Pierpont. The regiment's ten companies consisted of men from Wheeling, Parkersburg, Grafton and the counties of Wetzel, Taylor and Ritchie. Men from the Ohio cities of Ironton and Bridgeport and the Ohio counties of Monroe and Belmont, as well as Pennsylvanians from Pittsburgh, Greenfield and Washington County, also filled the unit's ranks. They spent the first year of the war guarding the Baltimore & Ohio Railroad at Clover's Gap. In 1862, they campaigned against Stonewall Jackson in the Shenandoah Valley under Major General John C. Frémont and then became part of Major General John Pope's Army of Virginia. The regiment saw action at Kelly's Ford in early 1863 and then returned to West Virginia. The 2nd West Virginia

Lieutenant Colonel Francis Thompson, commander of the 3rd West Virginia Mounted Infantry. *Ronnie Tront.*

suffered a defeat at Beverly on April 23, 1863, and remained there until Averell took command of the brigade. The unit was known to be "brave to the point of recklessness sometimes. It was said of [them] that whenever they got in a close place, every man was a general, and that they were almost invincible," as the regimental historian recalled. "They certainly achieved some victories that seemed in the beginning hopeless."[45]

Lieutenant Colonel Francis Thompson commanded the 3rd West Virginia Infantry (which was later redesignated as the 6th West Virginia Cavalry). Thompson, age thirty-five, hailed from Morgantown. In 1850, when he was twenty-two, he migrated across the continent to California and then on to Oregon. In 1855, he served as captain of Company A of the 1st Battalion of Oregon Mounted Volunteers in the Yakima Indian War, and from 1856 to 1857, he served in a battalion of Oregon and Washington mounted rangers against Indians, learning several Indian dialects along the way. He returned to Morgantown, where he worked as a potter, miller and justice of the peace.[46]

On May 28, 1860, Thompson was commissioned a first lieutenant in the 76th Virginia Militia. Governor John Letcher of Virginia commissioned Thompson a colonel and gave him authority to raise a regiment for the Southern service, but he refused the commission. Instead, he raised the first company for Union service in his county and was commissioned captain of Company A of the 3rd West Virginia Infantry in the summer of 1861. A few weeks later, he was promoted to lieutenant colonel. He was badly wounded at Second Bull Run but refused to leave the field until he toppled from his horse from loss of blood. He returned to duty in the spring of 1863.[47]

His regiment was organized in the vicinity of Clarksburg on July 1, 1861. The 3rd West Virginia was the second regiment raised under the call for troops to serve the Union and consisted of ten companies of men from the West Virginia counties of Monongalia, Harrison, Preston, Upshur, Taylor, Marshall and Ritchie and from the border area of southern Pennsylvania. It spent the first months of its service doing outpost duty in West Virginia and then joined Brigadier General Robert H. Milroy's command in the Shenandoah Valley in April 1862. It also fought against Jackson in the valley under Frémont's command and then fought at Second Bull Run. It performed outpost duty in West Virginia in September 1862 and remained there until Averell assumed command of the Fourth Separate Brigade in May 1863.[48]

Colonel John H. Oley, commander of the 8th West Virginia Mounted Infantry. *Steve Cunningham.*

Colonel John Hunt Oley commanded the 8th West Virginia Infantry (later redesignated as the 7th West Virginia Cavalry). Oley was born in Utica, New York, on September 24, 1830. Remembered as "a man of tremendous driving force," Oley was a merchant and telegraph operator before the war. In April 1861, he enlisted in Company H of the 7th Regiment of New York National Guard, a unit "in which every man was a trained soldier and fit to command." That summer, Governor Pierpont asked that six men of the 7th Regiment be sent to train West Virginia soldiers, and Oley was one of the men chosen. He organized the 8th West Virginia Infantry and was commissioned major in October 1861. He was promoted to lieutenant colonel on August 24, 1862, and to colonel on March 1, 1863. A friend remembered him as "a fine-appearing officer—intelligent, a good disciplinarian, and in every respect thoroughly qualified to command." The same friend also claimed that Oley "endeared himself to the officers and men of his regiment and had the respect and confidence of his superior officers."[49]

His regiment, the 8th West Virginia, was organized in Charleston in the fall of 1861. The regiment's ten companies consisted of men from the surrounding area. It served in the Shenandoah Valley against Jackson under Frémont and fought at Harrisonburg and Cross Keys. It also served in Pope's Army of Virginia as part of Major General Franz Sigel's corps.

Colonel James M. Schoonmaker, commander of the 14th Pennsylvania Cavalry. *Ronnie Tront.*

In November 1862, the regiment was first transferred to Colonel Augustus Moor's brigade and then was assigned to Averell's Fourth Separate Brigade in May 1863.[50]

Colonel James M. Schoonmaker commanded the 14th Pennsylvania Cavalry. Schoonmaker was born in Allegheny (now part of Pittsburgh), Pennsylvania, on June 30, 1842, the son of a wealthy drug and paint wholesaler. He was nineteen and was enrolled at Western University of Pennsylvania (now known as the University of Pittsburgh) when the war began. Already an accomplished horseman, he enlisted as a private in a local company that was mustered into the 1st Maryland Cavalry (U.S.). Within just a few weeks, he was promoted to second lieutenant and served in the August 9, 1862 Battle of Cedar Mountain. The young soldier had a difficult time adjusting to army life, as his colonel was a martinet.[51] However, as one biographer noted, "In all these positions he had shown the soldiership which led to his advancement."[52] He was a gifted guitar player and singer and often played for his men to prevent them from becoming homesick.[53]

That summer, he was sent to Pittsburgh to recruit a new cavalry battalion of five companies and filled the ranks of that battalion so quickly that he instead received authority to recruit a full regiment of twelve companies, to be called the 14th Pennsylvania Cavalry. In November 1862, at the precocious age of just twenty, Schoonmaker was commissioned colonel of the 14th Pennsylvania, making him the youngest colonel in the Union army. Secretary of War Edwin M. Stanton objected to the commission of such a young man as a colonel, but he nevertheless sent Schoonmaker on to Pennsylvania governor Andrew G. Curtin, who issued the commission.[54]

Those twelve companies were composed mainly of men from Allegheny, Fayette, Armstrong, Washington, Lawrence, Erie and Warren Counties and also included a detachment of men from Philadelphia. The new regiment mustered and trained in the Pittsburgh area and was then sent to Hagerstown, Maryland, where it received its full complement of horses and weapons. The men were trained in the various drills and evolutions of the

Major Thomas Gibson, commander of Gibson's Independent Battalion. *Library of Congress.*

line until they were garrisoned at Harpers Ferry in December 1862 as part of Brigadier General Benjamin F. Kelley's command. In May 1863, they were sent to Grafton, where they joined the Fourth Separate Brigade.[55]

Major Thomas Gibson Jr., age thirty-one, commanded Averell's Independent Cavalry Battalion. His father was the surveyor of the Port of Pittsburgh during the administration of President James Buchanan and also served as colonel of one of Pennsylvania's militia regiments. His mother came from a line of wealthy foundry owners, so he had a privileged life. Gibson was a graduate of Pittsburgh's Western University and was known as "a gentleman of culture and ability." One of his former soldiers remembered him as "always ready for a fight."[56] Another said that he had "inherited the Irish courage and daring."[57] He was originally commissioned captain of Company D of the 2nd West Virginia Infantry and was promoted to major of the regiment in July 1862. He resigned that commission in November 1862 to accept a commission as major of the 14th Pennsylvania Cavalry.[58]

By the summer of 1863, Gibson led a hodgepodge command composed of four companies of the 3rd West Virginia Cavalry, Captain Frederick Schambeck's Company C (known as the Chicago Dragoons) of the 16th Illinois Cavalry and the 3rd Independent Company Ohio Cavalry, raised in Cincinnati and known for "the energy and success with which it performed the work of scouting and screening."[59] The battalion was organized in Pittsburgh in June 1863 and was immediately assigned to join Averell's Fourth Separate Brigade.[60]

Captain Chatham T. Ewing, commander of Battery G, 1st West Virginia Light Artillery, shown in civilian attire. *Francis S. Reader,* History of the Fifth West Virginia Cavalry.

Captain Chatham T. Ewing commanded Battery G, 1st West Virginia Light Artillery. Ewing was born on January 30, 1839, near New Lisbon, Ohio. In 1852, his family moved to Pittsburgh. He became a member of the Pittsburgh Zouaves, an infantry militia company, in the summer of 1860. He was a tax collector and also studied law and was admitted to the bar in the winter of 1861; he had just started his own practice in Pittsburgh when war came. Known as "a splendid officer and a gentleman of culture," Ewing was commissioned captain of Battery G on August 2, 1861. Averell later described him as "an active, brave, and efficient artillery officer." The well-liked artillerist's battery consisted of two sections of two guns each, manned by western Pennsylvanians. The battery served with Frémont and Pope and then returned to West Virginia. Its men were veterans and were reliable.[61]

Captain Paul Freiherr von König, a German adventurer, commanded the detachment of the 68th New York assigned to serve with Averell's brigade. The twenty-three-year-old König, a baron and a member of an ancient ennobled family from Brunswick in Germany, had joined Averell's staff shortly before the Stoneman Raid and had remained there when Averell was sent to West Virginia. A small detachment of his regiment, the 68th New York, served with the Fourth Separate Brigade as a signal detachment. The precise size and makeup of this detachment is unknown, as it has not been documented. Baron von König's story is told in detail in Appendix B.

Once the decision to mount these men was made, Major General Robert Schenck, the commander of the Middle Military District, which included Averell's command, ordered the purchase of horses for the Fourth Separate Brigade. They were procured from Pittsburgh; Wheeling; Gallipolis, Ohio; and from the counties in the vicinity of the railroad running from Grafton to Parkersburg. In the rush to acquire sufficient mounts for the infantry regiments, any nag was purchased, meaning that the horses provided were of uneven quality.

Part of Averell's brigade was armed with an unusual weapon, the Lindner carbine. The Lindner carbine was a single-shot, .56-caliber breech-loading weapon that required a cartridge and an ordinary percussion cap. Approximately 501 guns and 100,000 cartridges were purchased by the War Department in December 1862 and were then issued to Averell's command, mostly to members of the 8th West Virginia.[62] The remainder of the Fourth Separate Brigade either received similar breech-loaders or their existing weapons were modified to fit them for mounted service. Averell then established a camp of instruction at Bridgeport, near Clarksburg, and on June 6, he sent the 3rd West Virginia there to drill. On June 9, he ordered the 8th West Virginia to go there as well. Horses were issued, but the necessary accoutrements were not sent with them. While waiting for the equipment to arrive, Averell instructed the officers in cavalry tactics.[63]

On June 15, the equipment finally arrived, along with orders to move to reinforce the Union command at New Creek, West Virginia, which was being threatened by the advance of General Robert E. Lee's Army of Northern Virginia, which was then in the process of invading Pennsylvania. The 14th Pennsylvania Cavalry met up with and joined the brigade on July 2, and the Fourth Separate Brigade helped to repulse a probe toward Beverly in Randolph County by the 19th Virginia Cavalry on July 4. After blunting the Confederate foray, Averell received orders to march his command to Webster, West Virginia, where it was entrained on the Baltimore & Ohio Railroad and transported to Cumberland to assist in trying to capture Lee's army, which was retreating from its defeat in Pennsylvania.[64]

These men were especially well suited to the travails that awaited them. "Averell's men were mountain bred and they took to the excursions that he laid out for them as to the manner born," observed one historian. "Where other commanders had made little circles like the rabbit, the army of Averell swung wide like the red fox. A thousand miles was just a pleasure jaunt for the Fourth Brigade."[65]

Averell received orders to advance from Cumberland to Hancock, Maryland, and arrived there on July 13 after a grueling fifty-mile march through rain and muddy, almost impassable, roads. His men then marched from Hancock to Williamsport, where they joined the main body of the Army of the Potomac about eleven o'clock that night. Averell and his brigade were in line and in position in time for its general advance on July 14. However, Lee's army had already slipped across the Potomac River to safety. The West Virginians missed their chance for glory when Lee's army escaped. However, other chances lay just ahead.[66]

When word came that Lee's army was retreating up the Shenandoah Valley toward Staunton, Averell received orders to return to the Martinsburg area. After sending patrols as far south as Winchester, Averell then received orders to march his command to Beverly, where it rested for a few days.[67] It needed that brief respite—a great adventure lay in store for Averell and his ragtag band.

2
For Want of a Nail
The Raid Begins

On August 5, Averell and his command of about fourteen hundred men left Winchester and marched twenty-eight miles over North Mountain to Wardensville. He had his entire brigade, less the 2nd West Virginia, with him. The Yankee horse soldiers passed through a gap in North Mountain west of Winchester and then moved into the Capon Valley.[68] The daring and intrepid Captain Paul von König, who led the brigade's way with a detachment of scouts, captured a captain and ten enlisted men and commissary supplies of Brigadier General John D. Imboden's Confederate cavalry brigade along the way. After resting for a few hours, the Fourth Separate Brigade covered another thirty miles on August 6, arriving at Moorefield at about eight thirty that night. That day, a detachment of the 14th Pennsylvania Cavalry was sent ahead to Moorefield via Harper's Mills. The Pennsylvanians captured a Confederate lieutenant and a few enlisted men. However, they fell into an ambush after dark, losing not only the prisoners but also thirteen of their own men captured by the enemy. Four of the Pennsylvanians were wounded, while three Confederates were killed and another five were wounded.[69]

The Fourth Separate Brigade spent a couple of days resting at Moorefield after covering nearly sixty miles in just two days. They moved out again on August 9, covering only eleven miles and heading to Petersburg, a small West Virginia town on the South Branch of the Potomac River. "My command was at this time badly in want of horse-shoes and nails, clothing, and ammunition, requisitions for which had been made by my quartermaster, at

Brigadier General Benjamin F. Kelley, commander of the Department of West Virginia. *Library of Congress.*

Cumberland, on the 7th," reported Averell at the end of the raid.[70] Averell decided to remain at Petersburg until the supplies arrived before he went on. And so the Fourth Separate Brigade sat and waited, losing the initiative with each passing day.

On August 12, Brigadier General Benjamin F. Kelley, who commanded the Department of West Virginia, sent orders to Averell. Kelley instructed Averell to move, without delay, to march to Huntersville in Pocahontas County, via Franklin in Pendleton County, to the Beverly and Staunton Pike, at or near Monterey, Highland County. Huntersville lay on the Huttonsville–Warm Springs road, fifty miles south of Huttonsville and twenty-five miles north of Warm Springs. Upon arriving at Huntersville, Averell was to attack Colonel William L. "Mudwall" Jackson's 19th Virginia Cavalry and drive the Southern horsemen out of the county. While passing through Pendleton County, Averell was to destroy the saltpeter and powder works there.[71]

Kelley instructed Averell to carry hardtack, sugar and bread and to gather beef and pork from the land along the way. Kelley told the New

Yorker to bring along any excess cattle for the use of the army and to give receipts for any supplies foraged from the countryside. Kelley also instructed Averell to impose stringent measures to prevent straggling by his command and also to prevent his troopers from interfering with private property rights along the way.[72]

Kelley indicated that he was ordering the 2nd and 10th West Virginia Infantry to join Averell's command upon his arrival at Huntersville, one of two towns in Randolph County and the county seat. He was to leave the 10th West Virginia at Huntersville, while taking the rest of the Fourth Separate Brigade on to Lewisburg to seize the law library of the court of appeals of Virginia stored there and then to bring the books to Beverly. "Great care will be exercised by the officer placed in charge that the books are not lost or injured," ordered Kelley. Once Averell seized the law library, he was to return to Beverly and report his arrival by telegraph.[73]

That same day, Kelley instructed Lieutenant John Rodgers Meigs, the son of the quartermaster general of the United States Army, Brigadier General Montgomery Meigs, to join Averell's staff as an engineer officer for the

Lieutenant John Rodgers Meigs, engineer officer assigned to serve with Averell's command. Meigs was the son of the quartermaster general of the U.S. Army. *United States Military Academy Archives.*

upcoming expedition. Young Meigs, a very bright young man who had just graduated from West Point a few weeks earlier, temporarily joined Averell's staff. He settled right in, reporting to his father, "Gen. Averills [*sic*] Staff and the Genl are very kind and very pleasant."[74]

Unfortunately, the necessary supplies still had not arrived. Averell did not believe that he could move without them, and he indicated that belief to Kelley. Kelley responded on the fourteenth, although Averell did not receive the note until the next day. "The assistant quartermaster informs me he sent you ten kegs of horse-shoes, which will arrive to-day; will send horse-shoe nails by the next train, and that he has ordered clothing for you from Wheeling, which he reports to arrive to-night," said Kelley. He told Averell that an infantry force under Brigadier General Eliakim Scammon would march from the Kanawha River Valley to try to join him at or near Lewisburg. Finally, he ordered that Averell should "move as soon as he possibly can. It is impossible to furnish Ewing with horses to mount his men for the expedition. You will move early in the morning and late at night, and rest your men and horses during the middle of the day." He concluded by stating, "The law library at Lewisburg was purchased for the western part of the State, and of course rightfully belongs to the new State of West Virginia. Our judges need it very much."[75]

Later that day, after receiving Averell's message, Kelley sent a second note. He informed Averell that he had ordered that salt be sent to his command and reported that he had also ordered cavalry pants to be sent for his men. "I am now after the ordnance officer with a sharp stick for the ammunition," he declared. "The nails will be sent as soon as they arrive." Kelley informed Averell that he had received a report that Jackson was near Huntersville with twelve or fourteen hundred men but that "he probably has about one-half that number." Because he could not supply Averell with any additional cavalry horses, Kelley instructed the New Yorker to seize them from the countryside and issue receipts for them.[76]

Some of the desperately needed supplies finally reached Averell at Petersburg on August 17, eight long days after the Fourth Separate Brigade had arrived there. The horseshoe nails and some ammunition for Ewing's guns were delivered but no small arms ammunition. "I was unable to increase my supply for small-arms, which amounted to about thirty-five cartridges to each man," reported Averell. "This was sufficient for any ordinary engagement, but we had a long march before us, entirely in the country

Averell's route of march.

occupied by the enemy, and I felt apprehensive that the supply would be exhausted before the expedition should be ended." In spite of this critical shortage of ammunition, Averell concluded that waiting in Petersburg for the delivery of more would be more dangerous than resuming the march with the supplies already on hand.[77]

Also on August 18, Averell sent Colonel John Oley and the 8th West Virginia up the North Fork of the South Branch of the Potomac River and Gibson's Battalion up the South Fork to scout. These men covered ten miles before camping for the night in a narrow strip of meadow with plenty of new hay and a good water source for the horses.[78] That night, Averell ordered the main body to be ready to march the next morning with three days' rations in their haversacks, along with grain for the horses.[79]

The 8th West Virginia covered twenty-eight miles the next day, crossing over Cheat Mountain in the process.[80] An officer of the regiment left a vivid description of the regiment's march that day. "The morning was clear and beautiful, with a pleasant breeze, and the men in the best of spirits," he wrote. "Besides we were passing through a settlement of loyal men, where they had organized a home guard, under the direction of an earnest and energetic leader. About the middle of the day we halted and watered our horses in the clear waters at the mouth of Seneca. Here we had the privilege of beholding one of Nature's wonders in the beautiful peaks of Seneca, that rise to the height of a thousand feet." The men paused to take in the lovely view of the valley below and then continued on their way.[81]

Ten days after arriving in Petersburg, Averell, with the 3rd West Virginia, the 14th Pennsylvania and Ewing's battery, marched toward Franklin, sending forward a couple of squadrons to destroy the saltpeter works five miles from Franklin.[82] The 8th West Virginia rejoined the main body of the brigade at Franklin. "As to our objective point we were all, except for the commanding officers, in the dark," groused one of Schoonmaker's Pennsylvanians.[83] After the long and frustrating delay, the expedition was underway again.

The men of the main body of the Fourth Separate Brigade were in the saddle by six o'clock on the morning of the nineteenth. "The order is given, forward, the long train starts; every man looks like he was on a pack horse going to market," remembered a trooper of the 3rd West Virginia. "Soon we are on the road to Franklin. The question now comes up, to what point of the compass are we steering? It is whispered among our men (who are not always asleep) that we are starting through the enemy's country, with a very limited supply of ammunition, horseshoes and nails, all indispensible to a successful campaign."[84] The intrepid horse soldiers pressed on through the summer heat and humidity, all the time wondering precisely what adventure lay ahead of them.

All along the way, bushwhackers took potshots at the marching Federals. The Federals "skirmished all the way with a double skirmish line right and left, and bushwhacked all night by murderous guerrillas," as a member of the 14th Pennsylvania Cavalry described the day's travails.[85] "The bullets sometimes came pretty close but it was rather better fun being in the advance than with the main body and so I was generally there," reported Lieutenant Meigs, who typically rode with General Averell and the rest of the staff at the head of the column when the Fourth Separate Brigade was on the move.[86]

On August 20, the Federals marched down the South Branch to Monterey, traversing a rough road while fending off bushwhackers and guerrillas. They captured a handful of the guerrillas along the way.[87] "They bushwhacked the trains in our rear and shot one poor fellow, a teamster in the small of the back," recounted Meigs. "I saw him today, he cannot expect to live. Another was wounded in the arm. It was rather a small kind of fighting however."[88] A member of the 14th Pennsylvania Cavalry recalled that the Yankee horse soldiers skirmished from daylight until dark and that "sometimes the enemy was so strong and aggressive that the whole command was deployed to resist his assaults."[89]

When the Federals arrived at Monterey, one of Averell's scouts, dressed in a Confederate uniform, was captured in the town, disarmed and placed under guard. When he did not return, the Union advance guard dashed into the town and stumbled upon a quarterly court-martial board that had convened there. The arrival of the Fourth Separate Brigade caused a hasty adjournment and the arrest of principal officers when one of the Yankee horse soldiers cried, "Halt!" As one Federal put it, "The court adjourned without ceremony, terror-stricken at the approach of the Yankee army."[90] The Federals released everyone but D.M. Anvill, who was the commonwealth attorney for Barbour County, a single military officer. Anvill had already done a stint as a prisoner of war at Camp Chase in Columbus, Ohio, and he glumly returned to captivity.[91] The jubilant Union men found salt, tobacco and other interesting parcels at the local post office that were divided up among the invaders.[92]

Averell was disappointed to learn that he had just missed capturing Major General Samuel Jones, the Confederate department commander, and Brigadier General John D. Imboden, who commanded a brigade of cavalrymen from West Virginia. Just the day before, Jones and Imboden had conferred at Monterey to discuss a plan for intercepting and attacking Averell's brigade.[93]

Knowing that the Confederate high command was preparing a warm reception, Averell proceeded cautiously on August 21. The Federals faced sharp skirmishing all day. "The march and skirmish were resumed and continued without interruption till we reached Greenbrier Valley," groused one of Averell's officers. "Here our picket lines were doubled and toward morning bushwhacked, then a skirmish line was thrown out, and the fighting was continued till daylight."[94] Two Confederates and one horse were killed. The blue-clads lost three wagons destroyed, six wagon horses killed and one wounded and three men wounded, including one mortally. The Federals bringing up the rear of Averell's column took some liberties along the way.[95]

"About nine o'clock we passed through a neighborhood noted for bushwhackers," recalled a member of the 8th West Virginia. "Here we burnt a mill, and the only mill destroyed in the expedition. Our advance had been fired into, and also our train, and from ten o'clock until two, we were fired into at several different places." That afternoon, when the Union horse soldiers stopped to water their horses, fifteen bushwhackers opened on them from above, picking off men and horses. "The cowardly scoundrels had placed themselves in such a position that it was impossible to reach them, and knowing that [they] were cavalry and could not lose the time to hunt them out, took advantage of this circumstance." The West Virginians made a mental note to come back and pay the bushwhackers another visit and dispense some retribution.[96]

"There goes one Yank on his horse, drinking cream out of a two gallon jar, his long beard is well besmeared. There another with tub of pickles standing on the front of his saddle dealing out to the boys. Another with a crock of butter or honey," recorded a member of the 3rd West Virginia. "Yonder are others going at full speed looking for horses, capturing &c. Soon the General

Lieutenant William H. "Will" Rumsey, aide-de-camp to Averell and commander of an expedition during the advance to White Sulphur Springs. *Ronnie Tront*

is apprised of the soldiering in the rear. Now you see a squad with drawn swords at every gate. Soldiers do not pass a sentinel; he is respected by the whole army."[97]

The blue-clad troopers took the road to Huntersville as far as the town of Frost, a distance of about twenty-four miles. Lieutenant William H. "Will" Rumsey, one of Averell's aides-de-camp, led the way that day, and his detachment ran into about three hundred troopers of Colonel William L. Jackson's 19th Virginia Cavalry.[98]

Jackson, a second cousin of the lamented Confederate hero Lieutenant General Thomas J. "Stonewall" Jackson, soon would earn the unflattering nickname of "Mudwall." Unlike his famous kinsman, William Jackson, a thirty-eight-year-old judge and prominent politician from Clarksburg, was not known for his military prowess. He was a big man, standing six feet tall and tipping the scales at about two hundred pounds. He had piercing blue eyes like his famous cousin and also had a shock of dark red hair.[99] One of his former soldiers remembered him fondly. "The fact is, he was as brave a man as lived, and never refused to fight, when the attendant circumstances were anything like equal," he claimed.[100] While Stonewall Jackson was most famous for his brigade's stand at the First Battle of Bull Run, Mudwall

A postwar image of Colonel William L. "Mudwall" Jackson, commander of the 19th Virginia Cavalry. *Library of Congress.*

Jackson was notorious for giving way.[101] A Confederate soldier explained the origin of the nickname: "We called him 'Mudwall' in contradistinction from Stonewall Jackson because 'Old Averill,' as we called Gen. Averill, always without an exception ran over him, knocked him down and ran him off."[102]

Jackson's large regiment came from the southeastern area of what became West Virginia, including Greenbrier County. His cavalry regiment was a new command, and poor discipline, straggling and absenteeism plagued it.[103] His company commanders had, until recently, been in independent commands, and they were not accustomed to taking orders or working together, and that significantly inhibited the effectiveness and efficiency of the regiment.[104] Jackson's primary responsibility was to secure the so-called Huntersville Line, which stretched for about thirty miles from southwestern Pocahontas County to Warm Springs in Highland County. Jackson also had a small detachment of infantry. His primary responsibility was to block any movement toward Staunton by Union forces, and he had deployed his forces accordingly. They were stationed in Highland and Pocahontas Counties, watching for activity along the Parkersburg and Staunton Turnpike and the Huntersville Road, and Jackson had to quickly call them back in order to try to block Averell's advance.[105] The question was whether this inefficient command would be able to halt Averell's advance.

Intelligence of Averell's raid reached Jackson almost immediately after the Federals marched again on August 18. Thus alerted, Jackson's detachments scouted the entire network of roads that could possibly be used by Averell. Although Jackson had the best possible intelligence regarding Averell's movements and intentions, he nevertheless proved to be ineffective at halting the advance of the Federal column.[106]

Rumsey's determined attack drove Jackson's hardscrabble troopers down the Knapps Creek Valley to the Northwest Passage, or Narrows, between Huntersville and Minnehaha Springs, a gorge in the mountains through which the Marlins Bottom and Warm Springs Turnpike passes, about five miles from Huntersville. There, Jackson's routed men fell back upon the main body of the 19th Virginia Cavalry, which held a position in a ravine, "and in that canyon a handful of men might hold an army."[107] Rumsey suffered four wounded and six horses killed and disabled despite being constantly annoyed by potshotting bushwhackers along the way. His command then bivouacked for the night, giving weary men and animals a chance to rest.[108] "Night comes and we camp on a Union man's farm," noted a West Virginian. "His hay, rye, oats, and corn are literally devoured. Such families should be remunerated."[109]

Averell determined that the ravine "was difficult to carry on account of the precipitous character of the sides," so he decided to feint with Gibson's Battalion on the twenty-second, while taking a byroad to the right with his main body. The main body reached Huntersville without meeting resistance, flanking Jackson out of his strong position in the ravine. Realizing that the Federals had flanked him and were about to get into their rear, Jackson and his cavalrymen beat a hasty retreat toward Warm Springs, leaving Huntersville in Averell's possession.[110] "His rear was fighting with our pickets. This we don't allow rebs to do, so the 8th [West] Virginia pursued them hotly, capturing five," recorded a trooper of the 3rd West Virginia, whose regiment drew up in line of battle but did not charge during this rear guard action.[111] "He was so much afraid of being cut off from W Springs that he left precipitously," noted Lieutenant Meigs.[112]

Jackson downplayed his rout. "Ascertaining my position at Gatewood's to be not so tenable as I had supposed," he wrote, "I moved my infantry that night to Jackson's River on the Warm Springs Road, leaving my cavalry a short distance below Gatewood's."[113]

The New Yorker sent Oley's 8th West Virginia and a squadron of the 3rd West Virginia in pursuit of the fleeing Confederates. "Heard of Rebels—but did not shoot any," reported a member of the 8th West Virginia in his diary that day.[114] The pursuing blue-clads caught up to Jackson's rear guard at Camp Northwest, driving them several miles before calling off the pursuit. Camp Northwest was the first elaborate camp to be built during the Civil War. It was located along the Warm Springs and Marlins Bottom Turnpike not far from Huntersville, and there were substantial log buildings as well as much equipment and supplies stored there.[115]

Averell's men burned Camp Northwest and destroyed its commissary buildings, stores, blacksmith shops, several wagons, a number of Enfield rifles, artillery equipment and a quantity of wheat and flour at a nearby mill. The Union troopers also seized a number of canteens, stretchers and hospital supplies that they found there.[116] The supplies were much needed. "We have lost a good many horses from exhaustion and have not found many for a remount as they are driven off when news of our advance arrives," observed Lieutenant Meigs.[117] Oley's loss was one man badly wounded—his leg had to be amputated.[118]

Having fulfilled Kelley's orders to drive Jackson and his cavalry from Huntersville, Averell waited for the arrival of the 2nd and 10th West Virginia. The 10th West Virginia, about 350 troopers of the 2nd West Virginia and a two-gun section of Captain John V. Keeper's battery arrived from Beverly on August 23. The men of the 2nd West Virginia were slightly better supplied than the rest of Averell's command—each man had forty rounds in his cartridge box, and they also had one thousand extra rounds with them that were distributed to the troopers of the 3rd West Virginia.[119]

The wait at Huntersville was not a pleasant respite for the Fourth Separate Brigade. "The fact was we had to fight the Johnnies continually all day to save ourselves from annihilation," remembered the historian of the 14th Pennsylvania Cavalry with a shiver. "Many of us wrote in our diaries, 'God only knows whether one of us will ever see home or friends again.'"[120] Another member of the 14th Pennsylvania said simply, "The command was engaged in a continuous skirmish."[121] Even though both men and animals needed a break from the travails of the campaign, this was not the sort of respite they had in mind.

"We have been dreadfully bushwhacked since we started on the trip," recounted a disgusted Major Hedgeman Slack of the 8th West Virginia, who had been left behind to take command of the dismounted men and sick horses when the rest of the Fourth Separate Brigade moved on. "They scarcely ever do much harm. They are so cowardly they keep so far away they are not very dangerous but they some times hit. I was especially marked out by one of them there one day and he took one fast shot at me but missed me by several feet."[122]

The men of the 2nd West Virginia had a difficult march from Buckhannon to join Averell. "It required three days to make the march, and we were beset by bushwhackers almost continually," recalled Samuel H. Knox. "Although we lost several men by this desultory fire, we could do nothing effectual to prevent it as the enemy were experienced mountaineers and always fired from some sheltered position, where all we could see of them was a wreath of smoke curling up among the rocks and bushes."[123] Another member of the 2nd West Virginia recalled it as "a very dangerous and exciting march." He noted, "We had considerable skirmishing, and our wagon train was attacked on the 21st, two of our men being wounded and several horses killed. The next day one of our command and two of the enemy were killed."[124]

Lieutenant Colonel John J. Polsley led a reconnaissance by a detachment of his 8th West Virginia toward Warm Springs on August 23. A few miles

Lieutenant Colonel John J. Polsley of the 8th West Virginia Mounted Infantry. *Steve Cunningham.*

into their march, they ran into about three hundred Confederate horse soldiers of the 19th Virginia Cavalry under command of Lieutenant Colonel William P. Thompson. "After considerable skirmishing assisted by one company of the Fourteenth Pennsylvania Cavalry and a company of the Third [West] Virginia Mounted Infantry, I drove them eight or ten miles," noted Colonel Oley in his report of the campaign.[125] The Federals captured a lieutenant and five enlisted men, probably of Thompson's regiment, while killing or wounding a dozen more. Polsley sustained only the loss of five horses on this excursion.[126]

Averell and his entire command, less the 10th West Virginia and the section of Keepers's guns, both of which remained on garrison duty at Huntersville, pursued Jackson in the direction of Warm Springs on August 24. "The march was continued first up the Alleghany Mountains, then through gorges, up and down, and over the mountain," recalled a Pennsylvanian.[127] After an ineffectual stand by the Confederate horse soldiers, the advancing Federals drove Jackson and his command through Rider Gap in Alleghany Mountain near Warm Springs in the direction of Millboro and near the state line.

Jackson dismounted about one hundred of the 20th Virginia Cavalry and ordered them up the slope of Alleghany Mountain to counter any flanking attempts by Averell. Part of this force crossed Back Creek Mountain via a footpath that terminated in Hidden Valley below. Averell's troopers chased the routed Confederates down this footpath. They captured "many arms, saddles, and other stores," reported Averell, at the cost of "2 men severely wounded, some slightly hurt, and a few horses shot." The panicked Confederates littered the roadside with saddles, bridles, guns, sabers and uniform parts as they fled.[128] The Fourth Separate Brigade camped at Bath Court House that night.[129]

Schoonmaker's 14th Pennsylvania Cavalry emerged from a dense fog and ran into an enemy picket post near Warm Springs. They captured all of the pickets, but an officer on a fast horse escaped and reported the advance of Averell's army. The 14th Pennsylvania then charged and surprised a strong enemy force and drove it up the mountain to where Jackson's main force waited. "Our boys fought bravely and many of them sold their lives dearly, but were overpowered by superior numbers and driven from the field," recalled the regimental historian of the 14th Pennsylvania. "Many were killed and wounded on both sides. Under a flag of truce we gathered up our fallen comrades, buried the dead, and cared for the wounded as best we could."[130]

With those minimal casualties, Averell drove Jackson and his cavalry right out of Pocahontas County and away from any opportunity to form a junction with any other Confederate forces that might have been operating in the area.[131] The Fourth Separate Brigade covered another twenty-five miles that day.[132] When the Federals entered Warm Springs, they learned that Mary Custis Lee, the wife of General Robert E. Lee, had left there just a few days earlier, hoping to escape from the coming Yankee horde.[133]

Jackson described the rout. "Observing that they were surrounding me, I fell back in time, for ten minutes afterward they surrounded the position I had occupied, and, discovering my retreat, rushed after me," he reported. "As the country between Jackson's River and Warm Springs Mountain gave their large force of cavalry the advantage, and as I knew there was a route to my left to Warm Springs which they could take and reach there before I could with my train (which was then but a short distance in my front), I fell back to Warm Springs Mountain, and placed my command in position for defense." Jackson assumed a defensive position there and waited for an hour until the head of Averell's pursuing column appeared in his front. "I soon saw that the effort of the enemy was merely to amuse me in front while he moved a force equal to mine in my rear and also on my right flank," recounted Jackson. After skirmishing for a few minutes, Jackson withdrew to safety several miles away, effectively out of the fight.[134]

A Confederate officer defended Jackson's conduct during Averell's advance. "Colonel Jackson was left alone to delay, as best he could, the progress of the enemy," recalled Lieutenant Colonel George M. Edgar, who commanded a unit assigned to Jones's department, "and though active, skillful, and persistent in his resistance of the advancing column, was successively flanked by the greatly superior opposing forces, and driven back beyond the Warm Springs, the Federal General's evident purpose being to create the impression that Staunton was the objective point of the expedition."[135]

Lieutenant John R. Meigs had a different take on the rout of Jackson's troopers. "We have by moving down from Petersburg to Franklin & Monterey and Huntersville occasioned a general skedaddle of all detachments in the Western Mts for fear of being cut off," Lieutenant Meigs told his father.

> *There are no troops but guerrillas infesting the Alleghanys & W of this place. Our information leads us to believe that all rebel troops intend to go East but that many of the soldiers will desert the army and take up bushwhacking rather leave the section to fight. We will we hope either capture or chase out of the Country all the rebel Force and the whole of W Va would then be in our possession if we choose to hold it.*[136]

The already challenging march grew even more arduous. The horses of the Fourth Separate Brigade were in bad shape, desperately needing horseshoe nails and some rest. And the surrounding countryside was buzzing with angry bees. "On our march which we hope will have been sort of a raking movement along the rebel line of outposts passing successfully in their rear we were a complete surprise as far as Monterey," observed Meigs. "The whole country is now however alarmed and up to bushwhacking."[137] Bullets buzzed along the column like so many riled-up hornets.

After determining that the prospect of overtaking Jackson was remote, Averell "determined to turn my column toward Lewisburg, hoping that my movement up to the Warm Springs had led the enemy to believe that I was on my way to his depots in the vicinity of Staunton." His troopers then made a rapid march of twenty-five miles to the important crossroads village of Callaghan in Allegany County, destroying the saltpeter works on the Jackson River as they went.[138] After arriving at Callaghan, Averell sent out reconnoitering parties toward Covington and Sweet Springs, capturing several enemy wagons near Covington and destroying the saltpeter works there.[139] This expedition meant that the Fourth Separate Brigade was now more than one hundred miles from its final destination at Beverly, whereas it had only been about fifty miles from Beverly while resting and awaiting the arrival of supplies at Petersburg. Its lines of communication and supply grew more attenuated with each step taken.

Along the way, Averell's command passed Warm Springs, where the Federals paused to enjoy the contrast of the warm and cold springs that flowed there. "It is a town of fine hotels, with both houses, gardens, shrubbery, arbors, and fine roads leading to it from the east, and but one good road leading west, and that to a resort of the same kind, the White Sulphur," recounted a member of the 8th West Virginia.[140]

The Fourth Separate Brigade camped at Callaghan, five miles from Covington, on the night of August 25, finding plenty of chickens, grain and other supplies for the taking. The weary, parched soldiers found a cool spring that produced sufficient volumes of water to fill the needs of the entire brigade but were shocked to find a guard posted at the spring to keep them away from it. "Soldiers, weary, worn and thirsty, must go to the creek and use the water out of which the horses drank," complained one.[141] "Here we waited until two o'clock in the morning," recalled an officer of the 8th West Virginia.[142]

While his weary men and horses rested, Averell reflected on the progress of his raid to date. So far, he had fulfilled every portion of Kelley's orders for the expedition. He had driven Jackson and two other Confederate forces out of Pocahontas County with minimal losses. He had destroyed Camp Northwest and its important supply depot, and he had captured supplies for his own use. He had captured Huntersville and had left a garrison there as ordered. So far, the expedition had gone flawlessly.

However, that was about to change dramatically.

3

The Confederates Respond

As Averell's column wound its way south, the "grapevine telegraph" buzzed with frantic activity, spreading word of the approach of the invading force across the countryside. As early as August 10, word filtered in that "the enemy [is] reported concentrating heavily at Moorefield to attack Staunton via Franklin and McDowell."[143] On August 18, General Robert E. Lee weighed in. He had correctly divined Averell's intentions and responded by instructing Major General Samuel Jones, commander of the Southwestern Department, to "threaten the enemy's flank, in making any movement through these passes, by a demonstration toward Huntersville, especially any approach via Monterey. I hope you will be successful in beating back any attempt he may make on your lines in the direction of Lewisburg."[144]

By August 23, "grapevine messages began pouring into the District Headquarters, then at Lewisburg, to the effect that Gen. Averell, with a large force of cavalry and artillery, was advancing from the northwest to raid the Virginia and Tennessee Railroad, which was one of the chief arteries for supplying the army of General Lee," remembered a Virginia artillerist.[145] Those grapevine messages—partly based on rumors—inflated the size of Averell's force to five to ten thousand effectives, the prospect of which sent a shiver up Jones's spine.[146] After hearing these reports, Jones concluded that the New Yorker and his mounted army were on a raid toward Staunton.[147]

Preventing Averell from severing the critical supply lifeline was crucial, and the Confederates were determined to pull out the stops to do so.

Major General Samuel Jones, commander of the Army of Western Virginia and Eastern Tennessee. *Library of Congress.*

"Celerity was absolutely necessary, for if General Averell should pass White Sulphur, there would be no force to prevent his reaching the railroad and doing immense injury to the line of transportation and communication between Richmond and Tennessee, and the country to the west," observed an early historian of the battle.[148] Even though the real object of the raid was unknown to the Confederates, they began making preparations to give the Fourth Separate Brigade a warm reception.

There was still a large degree of guesswork involved. "To know for sure the road Averell would take and be prepared to meet him on favorable ground was the momentous question with our commanding officer," noted the same artillerist.[149] Major General Samuel Jones was the commanding officer facing that challenge. Sam Jones commanded the Army of Western Virginia, which consisted of four brigades that operated largely independently. Jones, age forty-four, was a West Pointer. He graduated in 1837 and was an accomplished artillerist. He spent five years as an assistant professor of mathematics and as an assistant instructor in artillery tactics at West Point from 1846 to 1851 and then served as assistant to the judge advocate of the army until he resigned his commission on April 27, 1861, to accept an appointment as major of artillery in the military forces of Virginia. He was promoted to colonel and then was appointed brigadier general and chief of artillery and ordnance for the Army of Northern Virginia on July 22, 1861, the day after the First Battle of Bull Run. He commanded an infantry brigade for a time and then became commander of the Department of Florida. In May 1862, he was promoted to major general, and on September 23, 1862, he was appointed to command the Department of East Tennessee.[150]

Jones's geographic area of authority was uncertain. "Its boundaries, from the nature of things, were not clearly defined, but varied with the exigencies of the times," wrote Jones, referring to himself in the third person. "On September 1 [1863], his command extended from the vicinity of Staunton, in the Valley, to Saltville, in Southwest Virginia, a distance, as the crow flies, of about 200 miles, and by the traveled routes of nearly 300." Jones had fewer than six thousand total soldiers to defend such a large geographic area, a force "wholly inadequate for the defense of so extensive and important a country, from which a large part of the supplies for General [Robert E.] Lee's army was drawn, and a railroad of nearly 200 miles in length, the only line of transportation from East Tennessee through to eastern Virginia." The September 1863 returns for the Union Department of West Virginia, by contrast, showed approximately twenty-three thousand men present for duty.[151]

"He is about 45 or 50 years of age, I should think, about 5 ft., 10 inches in height, slightly built, light hair & sandy mustache and whiskers," a captain of the 8th Virginia Cavalry described Jones. "His expression is care-worn, and colorless. He is said to have distinguished himself by his bravery at the first battle of Manassas, and as he is a sensible man and understands his business, it is a pity for him that he should have been sent to this great western burial ground of military chieftains."[152] Jones was about to be tested.

Amiable forty-year-old Brigadier General John Echols normally commanded the First Brigade assigned to Jones's department. Echols, a Harvard-trained lawyer and politician, proved himself to be a competent soldier. He also suffered from serious health problems that plagued him throughout the war and prevented him from reaching his potential. Echols believed that he suffered from heart disease, which explains his frequent

Brigadier General John Echols, commander of Echols's brigade. Detached duty meant that Echols was not in command of his brigade at White Sulphur Springs. *Library of Congress.*

Colonel George S. Patton, commander of Echols's brigade at White Sulphur Springs. *National Archives.*

disability.[153] Consequently, his poor physical condition often prevented him from active duty and meant that he was seldom in command of his troops.[154] "He was not a field man," accurately observed Lieutenant Colonel George Edgar, who commanded one of the units in his brigade, "though an efficient organizer."[155] During the summer of 1863, he was detailed to serve on a three-man court of inquiry convened in Richmond by the Confederate government to determine why the critical Mississippi River bastion of Vicksburg fell to Union forces commanded by Major General Ulysses S. Grant on July 4, 1863. When Echols's disabilities or other duties prevented him from commanding his troops, his brigade's senior colonel, George S. Patton of the 22nd Virginia Infantry, ably led it in his place. Patton led the First Brigade so well that it was often called Patton's Brigade and not Echols's brigade.

Patton was born in Fredericksburg, Virginia, in 1833. He was the grandson of General Hugh Mercer, the Revolutionary War hero mortally wounded in action during the Battle of Princeton, and was the grandfather of his famous namesake, the World War II hero General George S. Patton Jr. He was tall and slender and had dark, curly hair and dark eyes. Colonel Patton graduated second in the Virginia Military Institute class of 1852 and then helped to found a private school in Richmond, where he served as assistant principal and taught mathematics and English, all the while studying law in the hope of joining the Virginia bar.

He married in 1856 and relocated his new family to Charleston, the eventual capital of West Virginia, where he started a law practice with a partner. He soon founded a volunteer militia company known as the Kanawha Riflemen. Ironically, Patton and William Woods Averell became social acquaintances during this period. Neither could then anticipate or appreciate the deadly waltz they would dance numerous times from August 1863 to September 1864.[156]

When war came in the spring of 1861, the Kanawha Riflemen became Company H of the 22nd Virginia Infantry. Patton was commissioned lieutenant colonel of the regiment and was ordered to report to Brigadier General Henry Wise's Army of the Kanawha. Patton was seriously wounded in action during the July 1861 Battle of Scary Creek, where he was left behind as too badly hurt to be moved.

After being exchanged, he eventually returned to duty and received a second serious combat wound near Giles Court House, in southwestern

Virginia, in May 1862. He was shot in the belly, and in those days, most gut shots were fatal. Patton himself believed that the wound was mortal, but a gold coin in his pocket saved his life by preventing the bullet from fully entering his abdominal cavity. However, he developed blood poisoning and had to go home to recuperate from his second serious combat wound.[157] He also learned that his exchange had never been formally completed, meaning that he could have been shot if captured again for violating his parole. Nevertheless, when Patton returned to duty, he was commissioned colonel of the 22nd Virginia.[158] Interestingly, three of his brothers also served as colonels of Confederate regiments.[159]

A friend described Patton:

> *His various and accurate learning revealed talents of a high order and of unusual versatility. To concentrate his thoughts upon a subject before him was natural and easy—not a laborious and painful exercise. Rapidly scouring the page, his eye would as quickly transfer to his mind whatever value it contained. Preferring the profession of law to any other business, and the sanctities of home and family to all other pleasures, he had, nevertheless, peculiar aptitude for a soldier's duty and a soldier's life. He enforced discipline without exciting dislike, and commanded his men without diminishing their self-respect. No private was ever denied the pleasure of conversation with his commander, and a courteous reception awaited all who chose to visit his quarters. When duty compelled him to deny a request, it was done with such evident reluctance, or with such kindliness of manner, that refusal gave less pain than is often suffered when a favor is granted with roughness or unwillingly.*[160]

George Patton would need all of his keen faculties if his slower-moving infantry brigade had a hope of defeating Averell's more highly mobile cavalrymen.

Patton's own 22nd Virginia Infantry was originally known as the 1st Kanawha Regiment from May to August 1861, when the name was changed. It consisted of ten companies of infantry made up of men who primarily came from the West Virginia counties of Kanawha, Putnam, Jackson, Nicholas, Monroe, Boone, Greenbrier, Roane and Wyoming. This command participated in almost every campaign in what became West Virginia, including the 1861 Kanawha Valley Campaign, the Battles of Cross Lanes and Carnifex Ferry, the 1862 Battle of Lewisburg and the 1862 Kanawha Valley Campaign, and

Lieutenant Colonel Clarence Derrick, shown at his 1861 graduation from West Point. Derrick commanded the 23rd Battalion of Virginia Infantry. *United States Military Academy Archives.*

also participated in the Jones-Imboden Raid during the spring of 1863. It was a hard-fighting, reliable, veteran regiment.[161] "It seems as if we always have to bear the brunt of battle in every fight [in which] we are engaged," wrote a member of the 22nd Virginia to his mother.[162] It "often campaigned in some of the worst possible geographic and environmental conditions, led by some of the most incompetent and incompatible generals the south could produce," observed regimental historian Terry Lowry.[163] With Colonel Patton commanding the brigade, Lieutenant Colonel Andrew R. Barbee was in command of the regiment.

Lieutenant Colonel Clarence Derrick commanded the 23rd Battalion of Virginia Infantry. Derrick was born to William Sharples Derrick and Ann Patterson Lyons Derrick in Washington, D.C., on October 7, 1837. His father was the chief clerk of the Department of State and occasionally served as acting secretary of state when circumstances demanded that he do so.[164] Clarence was educated at the school of Anthony Bolmar in West

Chester, Pennsylvania, from 1848 to 1853. He and his brother Henry Clay Derrick spent 1855 to 1856 surveying government land in Kansas, and then in 1857, Clarence Derrick was appointed to the United States Military Academy as a cadet. He graduated fourth in the West Point class of 1861 and then resigned his new commission in the prestigious Corps of Engineers after Virginia seceded from the Union.[165] He was commissioned a lieutenant of artillery in the Provisional Army of the Confederate States on March 16, 1861. That fall, he joined the staff of Brigadier General John B. Floyd, where he served until April 1862. On May 26, 1862, he was commissioned lieutenant colonel of the 23rd Battalion of Virginia Infantry.[166]

The 23rd Battalion, also known as the 1st Battalion or as Derrick's Battalion, was organized on January 15, 1862, with five companies under the command of Major David S. Hounshell. It was reorganized on May 21, 1862, and Derrick was placed in command. Three more companies were added in the spring of 1863, for a total of eight. Most of its men came from the southwest Virginia counties of Smyth, Tazewell and Giles; one company was from Mercer County in West Virginia; and one company came from Stokes County, North Carolina. The battalion's first action came in the 1862 Kanawha Campaign. White Sulphur Springs would be the battalion's second significant combat action.[167]

The 26th Battalion of Virginia Infantry was formed in the spring of 1862 when Captain George M. Edgar received authority to raise a battalion of infantry from the West Virginia counties of Monroe, Greenbrier and Mercer. Many of the men were veterans of the 59th Virginia Infantry who escaped capture at Roanoke Island, North Carolina, on February 8, 1862.[168] Company G of the 26th Battalion came from White Sulphur Springs and was known as the White Sulphur Rifles.[169]

Only three days after the battalion mustered in May 1862, the battalion fought in the Battle of Lewisburg, where the men broke and fled in panic, causing the 22nd Virginia to take heavy casualties and refuse to march with the 26th Battalion. Two new companies were added, and the battalion began redeeming itself during the 1862 Kanawha Campaign. One company, Company I, was formed in 1863 but was assigned to guard duty at the Confederate supply depot at Dublin, Virginia, and did not participate in the Battle of White Sulphur Springs.[170]

Lieutenant Colonel George M. Edgar commanded the 26th Battalion. Edgar was born at Union, Monroe County, West Virginia, on March 1,

A postwar image of Lieutenant Colonel George M. Edgar, commander of the 26th Battalion of Virginia Infantry. *Terry Lowry.*

1837. He graduated from the Virginia Military Institute in 1856, standing sixth in a class of thirty-three. He spent a year teaching in Union and then joined the VMI faculty as an assistant professor of chemistry. In 1859, Edgar became professor of natural philosophy and astronomy at the North Carolina Military Institute at Charlotte. In the fall of 1860, he resigned that position to become the chair of natural sciences for the Florida State Seminary at Tallahassee and was teaching there when Florida seceded from the Union in February 1861.[171]

He enlisted as a private in the Leon Rifles on April 2 and was immediately appointed sergeant. When the Leon Rifles were incorporated into the 1st Florida Regiment, Edgar was appointed sergeant major. However, his loyalties lay in Virginia, so he sought and received a discharge to go home to Virginia to raise a volunteer company in Monroe County. He was elected captain of that company, which joined the 59th Virginia Infantry. Edgar avoided being captured at Roanoke Island due to illness and sought authority to raise a battalion of infantry. He organized Edgar's Battalion on March 29, 1862, and was elected major. Edgar was seriously wounded at Lewisburg and was captured. When he returned to duty, he was promoted to lieutenant colonel of the redesignated 26th Battalion. Major General John C. Breckinridge later described Edgar as "a fine little officer."[172]

The 45th Virginia Infantry was also assigned to Patton's First Brigade. Former Virginia governor John B. Floyd, now a brigadier general in the Confederate army, was assigned to organize the militia companies of southwestern Virginia into an effective fighting force. He selected Henry Heth, a West Pointer, to organize and train these men at Wytheville, Virginia. The 45th Virginia was formed at Wytheville in May 1861 and consisted of men from Tazewell, Wythe, Grayson, Carroll and Bland Counties. Heth was the regiment's original commander. The new regiment consisted of ten companies and about nine hundred men.[173] Heth, who was a member of one of the so-called First Families of Virginia, hailed from the Tidewater region in the eastern part of the commonwealth. Heth was a strict disciplinarian who proved to be unpopular with the mountaineers serving under his command. The lack of literacy and discipline of his soldiers, combined with Floyd's lack of competence, frustrated Heth to no end. "I soon discovered that my chief was as incapacitated for the work he had undertaken as I would have been to lead an Italian opera," he declared.[174]

The 45th Virginia saw action at Carnifex Ferry, West Virginia, in 1861. That fall, after his unsuccessful Kanawha Valley Campaign, Wise was relieved of command and sent to Richmond for assignment, and Heth was promoted to general and took command of the brigade. Much of the regiment was reassigned to the 23rd Virginia Infantry. With the remnant of the regiment now under command of Lieutenant Colonel William E. Peters, the 45th Virginia participated in the Battle of Giles Court House. The regiment was then reorganized. Peters was not elected colonel and left the unit to assume command of a newly formed cavalry regiment, and William H. Browne became colonel of the 45th Virginia. The 45th Virginia also served in Heth's Kanawha Campaign of 1862, including the Battle of Lewisburg and then with General William W. Loring at Fayetteville and Charleston. The 45th Virginia spent most of the winter of 1862–63 guarding the crucial salt mines located around Saltville, Virginia. It was camped at Lewisburg when Averell's command approached and was tasked to defend the town.[175]

Colonel William H. Browne was born in Tazewell County, Virginia, on November 9, 1838, and was reared in Jeffersonville (now known as Tazewell). He attended Emory & Henry College for the 1854–55 academic year and then obtained an appointment as a West Point cadet in the class of 1861.

Browne resigned a week after the shelling of Fort Sumter in 1861 and never graduated. He was elected captain of Company G of the 45th Virginia on May 29, 1861, and was then commissioned colonel after the regiment's reorganization in May 1862.[176]

Captain Beirne Chapman's Company of Virginia Light Artillery, otherwise known as Chapman's Battery, also served with Patton's brigade. Chapman's Battery was raised in Monroe County, West Virginia, on April 25, 1862. Chapman had a hodgepodge of ordnance: one twenty-four-pound howitzer, two brass twelve-pound howitzers and two six-pound rifled guns. Chapman's guns participated in the 1862 Kanawha Campaign. The battery consisted of about 125 officers and enlisted men.[177] Captain Chapman, the son of General Augustus A. Chapman, was born on June 23, 1841, in Union, Monroe County, West Virginia. He was a bright student who attended Washington College in Lexington, Virginia, where he studied law. In 1861, while still a student at Washington College, he enlisted as a lieutenant in an artillery company, where he learned to be an efficient cannoneer. He resigned that commission and raised his own company on April 25, 1862.[178] When the battery marched to meet Averell's thrust, Chapman left two guns in Lewisburg and departed with the two three-inch rifles, one twelve-pound howitzer and the twenty-four-pound howitzer. Patton therefore had the same number of guns as Averell.

Patton's veteran brigade numbered about two thousand men. Although elements of other commands from Jones's department would help, Patton's men bore the brunt of the hard fight that was to come in just a few days.

Jones decided to try to corral Averell's column. On August 23, he sent orders to Colonel William H. Browne of the 45th Virginia Infantry. "If the enemy

The Gatewood Plantation house.
Pocahontas County Historical Society.

attempts to move on Colonel Jackson [at the lovely Gatewood Plantation near Mountain Grove in Pocahontas County, located twelve to fifteen miles from the county seat at Huntersville] by the road from Huntersville to Warm Springs…I think you can get in their rear, and you and Jackson together, perhaps, capture them." Jones gave Browne an accurate estimate of the size of Averell's force, telling him, "I do not think that Averell had more than 1,200 or 1,300 cavalry." He told Browne to take his orders from Jackson, even though Browne was senior to Jackson in rank, as Jackson knew the country well from years of operating there. "I trust that you two will manage

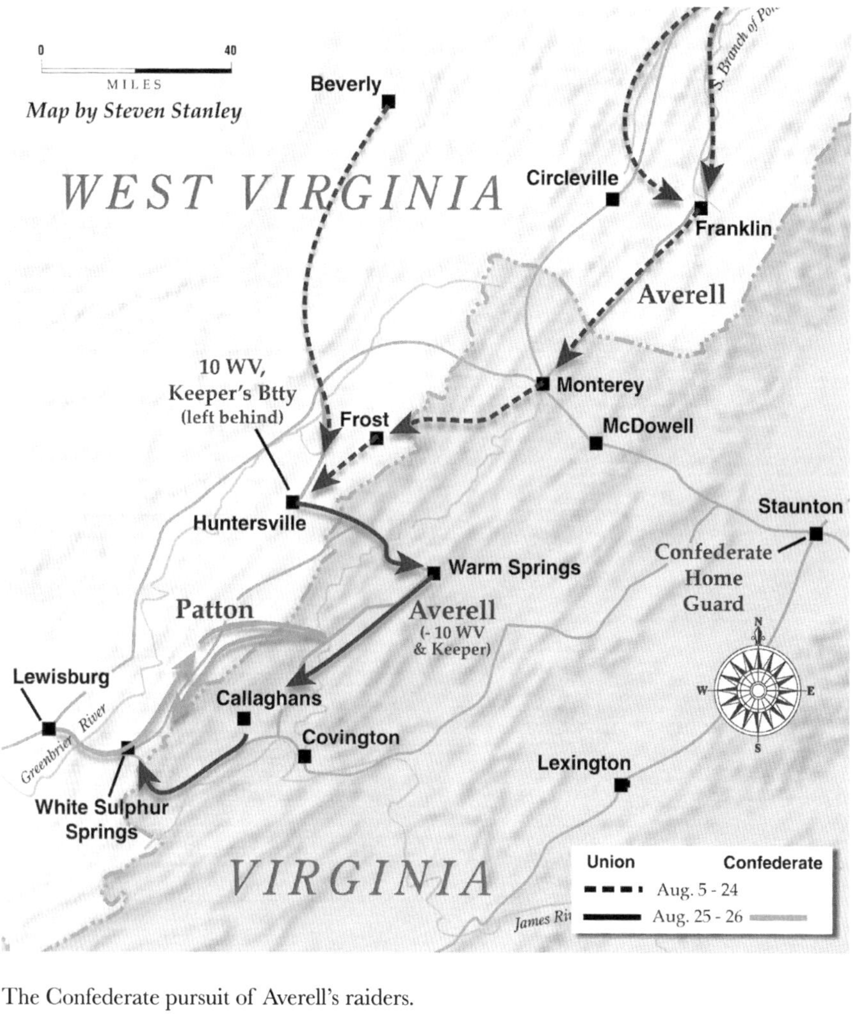

The Confederate pursuit of Averell's raiders.

as to punish the enemy severely before they extricate themselves from the mountainous country into which they have penetrated."[179]

He also ordered Patton to "move without delay…with your infantry and artillery, up Anthony's Creek, toward the Huntersville and Warm Springs roads, and co-operate with Colonel Jackson. Take with you one company of cavalry, leaving the remainder on the Frankfort and Pocahontas roads, to watch the enemy from that direction."[180] Jones now had all of the pieces in motion to try to intercept Averell. It remained an open question whether he would be able to do so.

On August 24, Sam Jones reported to the Confederate War Department that Mudwall Jackson and his cavalry had been driven from Huntersville. This came as an unpleasant surprise to Jones, who had ridden the roads with Jackson just a few days earlier and believed that Jackson's horsemen would be able to hold the position long enough to enable him to send a supporting force in time to help. "I have ordered such movements of troops from Lewisburg as I think will check them and frustrate their plans," he said. "I am apprehensive that the cavalry may be on a raid to the Virginia and Tennessee Railroad. I have no troops on that road." He then asked for reinforcements to garrison the railroad, including the brigades of Brigadier General Albert G. Jenkins (then commanded by the brigade's senior colonel, Milton J. Ferguson of the 16th Virginia Cavalry, as Jenkins had received a serious wound at Gettysburg) and Colonel Gabriel Wharton.[181] Although Robert E. Lee approved the transfer of these two brigades, Ferguson and Wharton were too far away and could not get there in time, meaning that Patton would have to make due with the troops he had at his disposal and could not count on reinforcements.

Jones also called out the Home Guard that day, sending them scrambling to defend the important railroad bridge over the New River. "Have your guns and ammunition issued to your company immediately," he instructed the commander of the Home Guard detachment at Wytheville. "The enemy's cavalry, 1,200 strong, are reported advancing on New River Bridge. Hold your command in readiness to move at a moment's warning."[182] As many as one thousand home guardsmen reported to defend the New River Bridge, and another two thousand men came out from Lynchburg in the direction of Lewisburg in an effort to bolster Patton's force.[183]

Jones also set Patton's brigade in motion from Lewisburg, with the task of stopping Averell's advance. Jones joined Patton and his foot soldiers on the

Anthony's Creek road on August 25. That morning, Jones received a note from Mudwall Jackson dated 9:00 a.m. the previous morning, indicating that Jackson had driven Averell's skirmishers back to his old camp near Huntersville. "The tenor of the dispatch induced me to believe that he could not only check the opposing force at Gatewood's but could move up and join [Patton's Brigade] at the intersection of the Anthony's Creek road from Huntersville to Warm Springs," reported Jones. "I dispatched him, informing him of the movement of that brigade, and directed him, if possible, to join it at the junction of the two roads above mentioned." However, Jones concluded that Jackson had never received the message and that the courier was captured.[184]

Uncertain of Averell's objective, Brigadier General John D. Imboden, who commanded the Valley District, called out the Home Guard in the Staunton area. Local citizens flocked to the armory in Staunton, where they were organized into an artillery company, two infantry companies and a company of Home Guard cavalry. "The whole town presented an attitude of defiance," reported a correspondent. "Men of over 60, with boys of 12 and 15, took their places in the ranks and shouldered shot-gun or rifle with alacrity. By mid-day, it was ascertained that…the danger was not so imminent. The people were dismissed with orders, however, to gather in the same organizations at a moment's call. Many seem to feel disappointment, mingled with relief, so keen had they become to meet the invading foe. This they will do, and I feel sure no small number of the enemy will find themselves able to reach our town. I learn that the country is also bristling in arms."[185]

Later that day, Jones learned of Jackson's rout by Averell. Still believing that the Federals' objective was Staunton, Jones ordered Patton to turn off from the Anthony's Creek road and take a shorter route to Warm Springs in order to meet the threat, meaning that Jones took Averell's bait and fell for the ruse. At the same time, Jones ordered Colonel James M. Corns and his five companies of the 8th Virginia Cavalry to march to White Sulphur Springs to intercept Averell.[186] He also ordered the local citizenry to remove their valuables, lest the Yankees plunder them.[187] The local citizenry fled from Warm Springs, "where great consternation had prevailed."[188]

"My comrades who were on that march will recall the haste in which this order was executed, the silence enjoined on officers and men, who in a high state of expectancy, rivaled 'Jackson's Foot Cavalry' in the rapidity with which they covered the ground," remembered Lieutenant Colonel George M. Edgar of the 26th Battalion of Virginia Infantry. In the evening, they bivouacked "on a brushy slope…which after they encountered formidable dens of snakes, [and] eating a hasty meal, were soon in profound slumber." The men of Patton's command still had no idea what emergency faced them.[189]

Conflicting reports swirled. A telegraphic dispatch from Staunton claimed "that the Yankees are falling back, which is very probable, as [the Northwestern Cavalry Brigade, commanded by Brigadier General John D.] Imboden is on their track. Their object seems to be the destruction of the [Virginia] Central railroad."[190] This sort of speculation only further muddied the waters as the Confederate authorities grappled with trying to ascertain the true objective of the invasion.

About ten o'clock that night, Jones learned the truth: that Averell was advancing from Warm Springs toward Callaghan—in other words, that the Union horsemen were going the opposite way. "I immediately ordered Colonel Patton to return on the Anthony's Creek Road in the hope of intercepting the enemy on the road from the Warm to the White Sulphur Springs." Word reached Patton's bivouac about two o'clock that morning. By a forced night march, the Virginians marched to the mouth of Anthony's Creek, crossed the Greenbrier River Bridge and came out on the road to White Sulphur Springs. They then turned onto the Midland Trail, with Edgar's troops leading the way.[191] After nearly twenty-four straight hours on the road, the Virginia infantrymen were within a mile and a half of the crucial road intersection. The advance guard reached the intersection just in time to meet the advance of Averell's column on the morning of August 26.[192]

The intersection of the James River Turnpike and the Anthony's Creek Road, which was the center of the battlefield. The small house had a cannonball hole in it from a Union artillery shot. *West Virginia State Archives.*

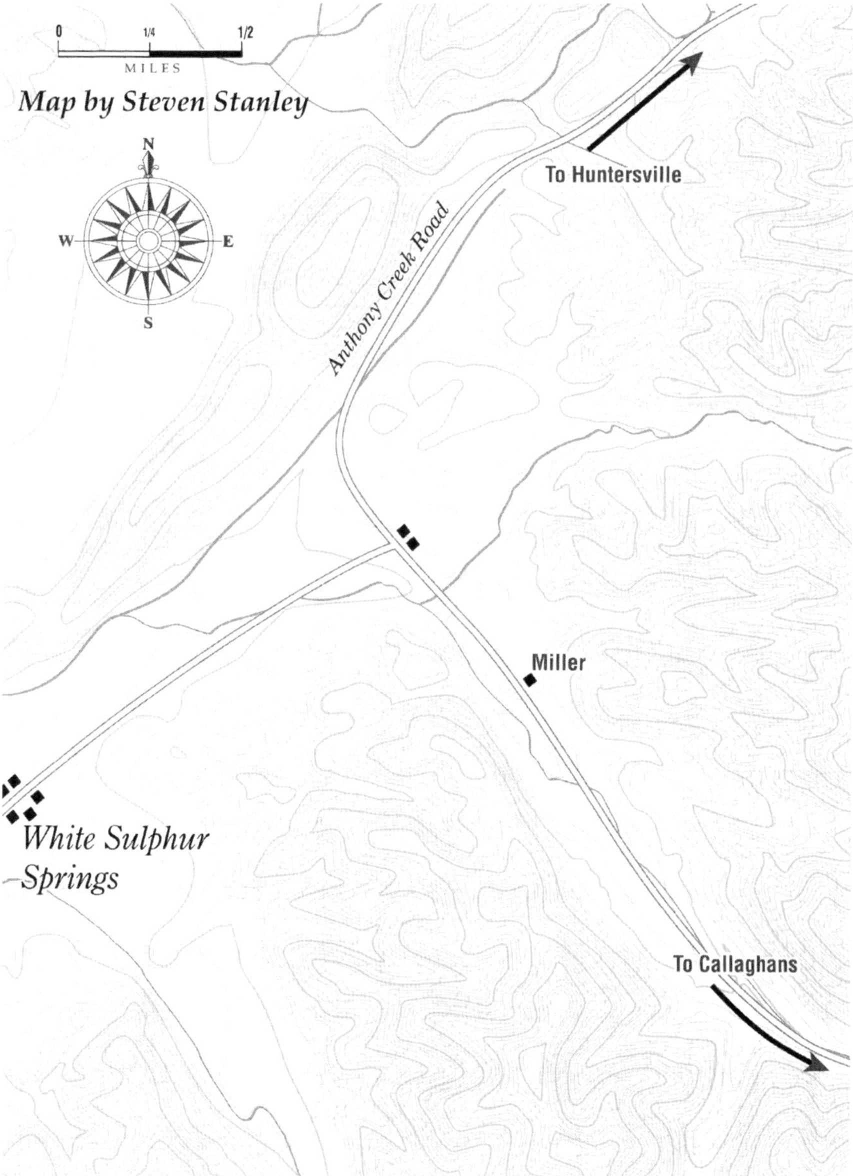

The White Sulphur Springs battlefield.

"What was the matter? Were we pursued or pursuing, or trying to head off the enemy in the other direction?" recounted Edgar. "We could only conjecture. One thing was plain—there was great urgency governing the movements, for though sleepy and but little rested, our speed was increased and the steps were short." He continued, "Couriers came and others went, but no changes were made either in the direction or speed of the march."[193] One of Patton's infantrymen correctly observed, "If we had been one half hour later the Enemy would of passed on to Lewisburg and gotten away without a fight."[194]

After leaving the 23rd Battalion of Virginia Infantry and the 37th Battalion of Virginia Cavalry behind at the nearby Greenbrier River Bridge, Jones rode out to meet up with the rest of Patton's Brigade. Jones sent two of his staff officers, Adjutant Noyes Rand and Major George McKendree, to ride ahead while Jones and the rest of his staff rode about a mile to the Dry Creek Hotel. Charles W. Humphreys of the 26th Virginia was part of the advance guard, watching as the battalion marched by. Just then, a panicked Rand galloped back, crying out, "Clear the road; the Yankees are coming!" He reported that the blue-clad troopers had captured McKendree, and he "had gotten away by the skin of his teeth." Noyes then dashed away as fast as his horse could carry him to report to Jones that the enemy was coming in force. "In about ten minutes the General and his staff came back riding a la Sheridan twenty miles away, minus the poetry," remembered Humphreys.[195]

What became the White Sulphur Springs battlefield is approached by a narrow gorge, traversed by two major thoroughfares, the James River and Kanawha Turnpike and the Anthony's Creek Road, which intersected with the turnpike about the middle of the valley. These two roads were nearly at right angles with each other. A small wood-frame house stood at the road intersection, and several other houses dotted the battlefield. The gorge opened into a gently undulating valley that was bounded on the right by a hill that was wooded at the top but cultivated as a cornfield at the bottom. The hill gently sloped toward Wade's Creek, which in turn was bounded by precipitous bluffs that were covered by scraggly cedars and other mountain growth. The terrain favored the defense and meant that this intersection could not be flanked; only a successful frontal attack would drive the defenders from the intersection. The town of White Sulphur Springs lay about a mile to the west, and a small settlement centered on the house and store of a prosperous local merchant named Henry Miller. This valley became the scene of the heavy fighting that would occur the next day.[196]

The pieces were now all in place for the Battle of White Sulphur Springs. Would Patton be able to stop Averell from reaching Lewisburg and the law library?

4

The Battle Is Joined

At four o'clock on the morning of August 26, Brigadier General William W. Averell formed his Fourth Separate Brigade to move out in the direction of White Sulphur Springs. It proved to be a bright, beautiful summer day, ideal for fighting a battle.[197] The intrepid Captain Paul Freiherr von König led the way with the advance guard of two companies of the 2nd West Virginia and two companies of the 8th West Virginia. Next came the balance of the 2nd West Virginia, followed by the balance of the 8th West Virginia. Gibson's battalion was next in line in the column, followed by Ewing's battery, the 14th Pennsylvania Cavalry, with the 3rd West Virginia bringing up the rear of a column that stretched for four miles.[198] The Federals encountered two mountain ranges in the first ten miles of the march, slowing the pace of their advance significantly. "After passing the summit of the mountain we dashed down the ravine at a trot," recounted a member of the 8th West Virginia.[199]

Lieutenant Alexander J. Pentecost, the quartermaster of the 2nd West Virginia, rode with Captain Chatham T. Ewing, Averell's battery commander. While the two officers chatted about various subjects, they spotted a man on a gray horse descending a hill. As soon as the man spotted the advancing Union troopers, he turned tail, put spurs to his horse and tried to flee. Ewing and Pentecost galloped off in pursuit and soon overtook and captured the man. In reply to Ewing's questions, he admitted that he was a Confederate quartermaster officer and was out purchasing supplies.

Lieutenant Alexander J. Pentecost, quartermaster, 2nd West Virginia Mounted Infantry. *Frank S. Reader,* History of the Fifth West Virginia Cavalry.

Ewing spotted something bulky in the man's pocket and asked what it was. "It is Confederate money," the man replied, pulling out a large wad of bills, which Ewing promptly seized. The man asked for a receipt so he could account for the money, and Ewing replied, "This is our quartermaster and he will give you a receipt." With that, Ewing wheeled and rode off, leaving Pentecost to deal with the man, who was handed over to the brigade's provost marshal.[200]

By 9:30 a.m., Averell and the main body had only covered thirteen miles. However, Baron von König and his advance guard had already arrived at Rocky Gap and had already faced stiff resistance from Patton's Virginians. The baron sent a note back to inform Averell that the enemy was in his front in force and that he needed reinforcements. Averell ordered a squadron of the 2nd West Virginia to advance at the trot, and he also dispatched a squadron of the 8th West Virginia to support them. A few minutes later, Averell heard Chapman's guns barking, announcing George Patton's "purpose of disputing our farther progress and indicated his strength."[201]

After an exhausting all-night march, Patton's advance guard—Lieutenant Colonel George Edgar's 26th Battalion of Virginia Infantry—reached and then passed the intersection of the Anthony's Creek Road and the James River and Kanawha Turnpike just as Baron von König's advance elements began emerging from the Rocky Gap gorge. In short, the Virginia infantrymen got there just in the nick of time. Patton ordered Edgar to countermarch his men and form them in line of battle across the road, facing eastward, and to deploy a company of skirmishers to his left and front.

Edgar formed four companies on the left of the intersection of the two roads and sent Major Richard Woodram with the other four companies to

A view of the center of the battlefield. The road intersection where the Confederates built their barricade is in the center of the photograph. *West Virginia State Archives.*

the right, forming along the edge of the woods.[202] "To place the battalion in a defensive position on elevated ground on the side of the turnpike is the work of but five minutes, where with loaded arms it awaits developments," recalled Edgar.[203] Patton also ordered Edgar to hold on until the rest of his brigade arrived, giving Edgar a stern task.[204]

Patton also sent one of his staff officers, Lieutenant J.W. Branham, on a reconnaissance into Averell's rear to find out how large a force was approaching. Branham dashed off and successfully completed the ride, reporting the results to Patton just as the Confederate infantry took position. The critical intelligence that Averell's entire brigade was advancing told Patton how he needed to deploy his troops to meet the threat.[205]

Edgar's men used the few minutes available to them to cobble together a crude barricade across the road. The hastily built barricade was just strong enough to hold off the initial Union attacks and to deceive the Federals as to its strength, and Edgar's men stood long enough for the rest of Patton's Brigade to come up and deploy. "The enemy were strongly entrenched," recorded a member of the 2nd West Virginia.[206] However, Patton had chosen the position well—because of the high ground on either side, it could not be flanked, and if Averell were to drive the Confederates off, he would have to do so by frontal assaults.[207]

Edgar had no idea how large of a force he faced that morning. He never realized that Averell had only thirteen hundred carbines in his brigade. Just a few days after the conclusion of the battle, Edgar wrote to the commandant of the Virginia Military Institute and stated his belief that "the enemy's force

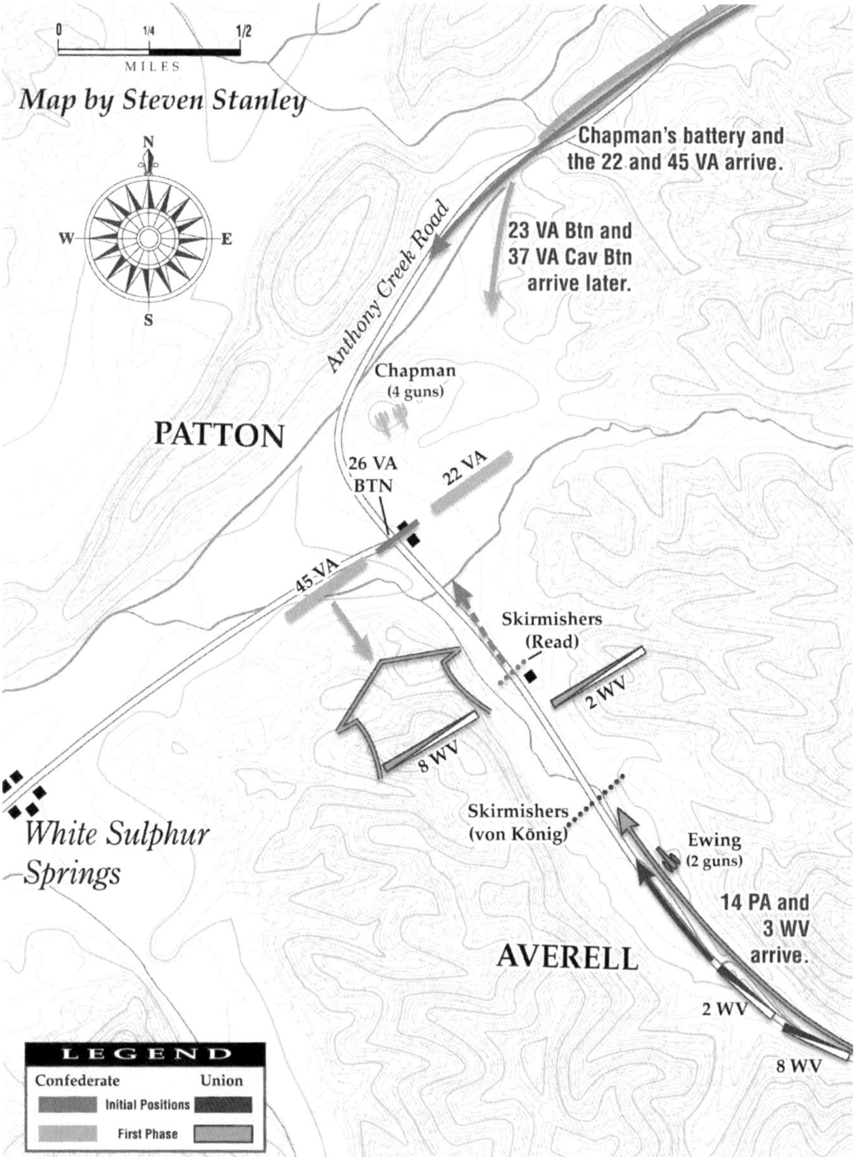

The battle opens, morning, August 26, 1863.

was not less than 4,000."[208] Edgar, convinced he was badly outnumbered, nevertheless vowed to execute Patton's orders.

The company of skirmishers, under command of Captain Edmund S. Read, advanced to the house and store of Henry Miller, situated about one

A postwar image of Captain Edmund S. Read, who commanded a company of the 26th Battalion Virginia Infantry. *Terry Lowry.*

hundred yards in front of Edgar's left. Read and his soldiers opened the battle by unloosing a volley at von König's column that halted the German baron and his two companies in their steps and drove them back.[209] However, the Federals "soon reappeared in skirmish line and we began the practice of taking pop shots at them," recalled a member of Read's Company B of the 26th Battalion. "The situation was looking quite stormy for us when Chapman's Battery broke loose behind us and sent our foes scampering back for a while."[210]

Patton and his staff sat on a nearby knoll, watching Edgar's battalion fend off the initial Federal attacks. Seeing Averell's initial assaults fall back, Patton exclaimed, "Glorious! Hurrah for the gallant Edgar!" and then asked his adjutant, Lieutenant Noyes Rand, to carry his compliments to Edgar. Rand deferred to Lieutenant Colonel David S. Hounshell, who was temporarily serving as a volunteer aide that day. Hounshell rode deliberately across and toward the line of fire in a diagonal direction, "as if on dress parade," as Rand remembered it. Edgar rose to receive the message, exposing himself to heavy enemy fire as he did so. "None of us of the Staff envied Edgar the ordeal of receiving a set speech under a rain of bullets."[211]

Soon after daylight, while they were about a mile and a half from Dry Creek, a courier from Colonel Patton reached Captain Beirne Chapman,

Left: Lieutenant John P. Donaldson and Adjutant Noyes Rand of the 22nd Virginia Infantry. Rand served as Colonel Patton's adjutant when Patton was in brigade command. *Louise Testerman Collection, Virginia Polytechnic Institute.*

Below: The Confederate artillery was located on the high ground to the left, and the Union artillery was located on the high ground to the right. *West Virginia State Archives.*

bearing a dispatch. After reading the urgent message, Chapman ordered his men forward at the double-quick, "as fast as horses could trot with a battery." They arrived at the intersection of the Anthony's Creek road and the turnpike just as Averell's line of battle began advancing.[212]

Patton ordered up the four guns of Chapman's battery and deployed them to the left of the Anthony's Creek road and on a knoll behind Edgar's battalion. The Southern gunners opened at the advancing Federals, scattering von König's scouting parties. "We immediately opened on their columns," reported Chapman, "firing slowly and deliberately."[213] Sergeant John G. Stevens, one of Chapman's artillerists, proudly recalled, "Chapman's battery opened fire at once, and was given the credit of holding back the enemy long enough for our infantry to form in line of battle. I never saw our men so greatly excited, while we were getting into position shells were bursting among us, and the minie [*sic*] balls singing like August crickets."[214]

Captain Read then ordered his company to charge, and some did, but "most of them thought to let well enough alone," recalled C.W. Humphreys of Company B. "So he and those of us who followed him walked quietly back, our captain coolly remarking, 'It was not as good a place as I thought it was.'" Humphreys, in a masterpiece of understatement, agreed. "It certainly was not a good place," he said. Read then pulled his company back to his left rear, leaving a gap between them and the road for the deployment of Company H of the 22nd Virginia. "There was a deep hollow in our front, as we took position behind a fence that ran down a lone ridge," recalled Humphreys. "In our immediate rear was a steep place, at the foot of which was cleared land extending back some two hundred yards. We were in this position when the storm broke loose."[215]

Patton also ordered the 22nd and 45th Virginia Regiments to come up and form a line of battle, with the 22nd on the left of the battery and the 45th

The Confederate viewpoint as Patton's brigade approached the battlefield. *West Virginia State Archives.*

on the right.[216] Patton ordered both regiments to hold their positions at all costs, since they represented the center of the Confederate line.[217] When the 45th Virginia deployed, Edgar pulled back one of Woodram's companies and placed it on his left, leaving only three companies with Woodram on the right.

The 45th Virginia extended its line across the low ground to the base of the ridge on the right. Captain William H. Thompson led one hundred men of the 45th Virginia to occupy a knoll to the right of the main line of battle that Patton was cobbling together. Colonel William H. Browne, commander of the 45th Virginia, had his men throw up a hasty barricade of fence rails, and they took position behind it.[218]

Hearing the firing break out at the intersection ahead, Averell immediately started his entire column forward at "a rapid gait" down into and through the narrow gorge of Rocky Gap. The whole column advanced "as rapidly as the nature of the ground would permit," noted one of Averell's men.[219]

Captain Francis Mathers of the 8th West Virginia Mounted Infantry. *West Virginia State Archives.*

"We found a little grove of sugar trees and dismounted and appointed details to hold the horses," recalled Captain Francis Mathers of the 8th West Virginia. "Our regiment was ordered to charge upon the rebels on the left, and dislodge them from that position," while the 2nd and 3rd West Virginia and 14th Pennsylvania attacked on the right.[220] "Thus formed, the federal soldiers sent the messengers of death among the rebels like hail stones and fire," colorfully noted a member of the 3rd West Virginia a few days after the battle.[221]

"The fight soon became general and terrific," remembered a member of the 3rd West Virginia. "Balls, shells, grape and shot flying with fearful havoc in all directions, doing the work of death. The whole atmosphere resounds with the roar of artillery and musketry…For four or five hours I believe there was not an intermission of more than two minutes at any one time—almost an incessant fire."[222]

William Marshall Dearing served in Company F, 3rd West Virginia. When Chapman's gunners opened on their advance, a Confederate cannonball rolled down the hill, headed directly for Dearing's position. The man next to Dearing thought he could stop the cannonball by just sticking his foot out. The man stuck his foot out, but his doing so not only failed to stop the cannonball's momentum but also snapped the man's foot in two, causing him to collapse, shrieking in agony. Dearing and another soldier dragged the injured man back to safety while under heavy enemy fire. When they advanced again, the men of the 3rd West Virginia came so close to the enemy line that they could see the faces of the Southerners. The West Virginians received orders to lie down in the creek bed and wait for the order to attack.

Averell's command approached the battlefield from this narrow gorge. *West Virginia State Archives.*

Dearing recalled, "The bullets whizzed all around us like angry bees, and kicked up little puffs of dust as they hit the dirt all around us."[223]

As the head of the Union main body emerged from the gorge, Chapman's artillery shells rained down. The sheer cliff on the right offered some protection for the horses of the dismounted men of the 2nd and 8th West Virginia, who deployed. Averell ordered the squadron of the 2nd West Virginia to climb to the top of the ridge to the right and a squadron of the 8th West Virginia to deploy on the top of the hill to the left of the gorge.[224] He also brought up a section of Ewing's battery, which immediately unlimbered and began trading counter-battery fire with Chapman's guns, quickly dismounting one of Chapman's rifled guns with its accurate and deadly fire.[225] Averell then established his headquarters just behind Ewing's guns and remained there for the rest of the day, directing the movements of his troops from that position.[226]

Unfortunately, the 8th West Virginia somehow mistook the direction and, instead of going to the left, went to the right with the 2nd West Virginia, leaving the hill to the left of the gorge temporarily undefended. Colonel Oley and the balance of the 8th West Virginia then came up and made their way to the crest of the hill on the left. Oley reported, "We immediately dismounted and double-quicked up the hill. The enemy was found in possession of the crest of the hill, but such was the gallant and impromptu charge of my men that we quickly drove them down the hill with great confusion, killing several and wounding a number."[227] The speed of the attack prompted a member of the 8th West Virginia to claim that the regiment "fought the rebels rapidly."[228]

Colonel Oley lamented the loss of two brave officers in this charge. Lieutenant John A. Morehart, a German immigrant, was killed instantly while scaling the hill when a rifle ball entered his skull through his eye socket. Captain William L. Gardner of Company E, whose company had the right of the 8th West Virginia's line and connected with the left of the 2nd West Virginia, was killed instantly by a sharpshooter's ball that passed through his head.[229] These two young men were "highly esteemed as honest, worthy men," lamented their hometown newspaper in Gallipolis, Ohio. "From what we know of the men, their courage, energy and honorable bearing as soldiers, there is no doubt, they died as only the brave can die."[230] In addition to these two officers who were killed, the 8th West Virginia suffered several other casualties during the attack on the hill.[231]

Patton's men counterattacked a few minutes later, and "although I had to retire a little, they gained no material advantages," reported Oley. However, the colonel lost another company commander during this counterattack. Captain William H.H. Parker, who commanded Company H of the 8th West Virginia, was wounded and captured when Oley was forced to leave the wounded officer on the field.[232]

Averell also ordered the 3rd West Virginia and 14th Pennsylvania to come up and deploy, but it took time for them to do so with the column strung out in a narrow gorge for four miles.[233] The inevitable delay of the deployment of the 3rd West Virginia and 14th Pennsylvania meant that Ewing's guns did not have as much support as they should have had. When Edgar's battalion attacked, "the Second on the right, and the Eighth on the left, afforded some support, but Ewing's battery, with canister, not only resisted the approach of the enemy, but actually advanced upon him, in order to obtain a better position," reported Averell, "and held him at bay until the arrival" of the 14th Pennsylvania and 3rd West Virginia, which were immediately deployed on the right and left of the turnpike, plugging the gap in Averell's line.[234] The 14th Pennsylvania held the right end of Averell's line, with its Company A anchoring the far right flank of the Union line.[235]

Ewing was searching for a better position for his guns when he came under fire. Averell arrived at the front just in time to see Ewing fall, badly hurt. "I saw him fall desperately wounded in the thigh or hip, with great fortitude he kept his place, that is, continued for some time to direct the operations of his gunners until the onset of the enemy was repelled," recalled General Averell.[236] Adam Brown, who served under Ewing, was also desperately

Lieutenant Howard Morton, who assumed command of Ewing's battery after Ewing was severely wounded in combat. *Ronnie Tront.*

wounded at Ewing's side during this vicious exchange, eventually losing an arm to his injury.[237] The unconscious Ewing was carried from the field, and the battery's senior lieutenant, twenty-one-year-old Howard Morton, took command.[238] Morton, described as "a brave officer and thoroughly qualified for the position he held," handled the battery with skill and aplomb for the rest of the engagement.[239]

Morton's two guns wreaked such havoc on Chapman's battery that Chapman galloped up to Sergeant John G. Stevens, who commanded one of his guns, and asked, "That cannon is tearing us all to pieces; can't you do something?"

"I do not know where they are," replied Stevens.

"Turn around and fire there on the mountain," responded Chapman, "and make them think you know where they are." Stevens yanked the lanyard and a shot belched forth from his gun. The Union gun did not respond, largely because its tube had burst at the muzzle.[240]

Richard Minner of Chapman's Battery was lying behind a tree stump when a piece of Union shrapnel ripped into his thigh, badly shattering the leg and severing the femoral artery. Minner lay in a pool of his own blood. Stevens saw the injured soldier and, at great risk to his own life, went to Minner and carried him to safety in the rear under heavy fire. Unfortunately, Minner was mortally wounded, and the Southern surgeons could only ease his pain until he died.[241]

When Lieutenant Morton ordered the two Union cannons to relocate, Chapman's guns threw shells and canister at them, spooking the battery horses, which reared and broke the pole of one of the guns. That, in turn, drove the cannon off the road, and then the limber got hung up on a stump, stranding the gun there. A sergeant ordered the drivers to turn their horses and pull the gun back on the road, which they did with serious loss while taking heavy fire from Chapman's guns. A new pole was inserted into the gun, and it soon went back into action, once more belching fire at the Confederates.[242]

Repulsed by the severe fire of Morton's two guns, Edgar's men retreated to their barricade. "The enemy gave away his position to us, and endeavored to assume another about half a mile in rear of the first, with his right resting upon a rugged prominence, his center and left protected by a temporary stockade, which he had formed of fence-rails," stated Averell. "I resolved to dislodge him before he should become well established, and then, if possible, to rout him from the field."[243]

When Edgar's battalion fell back, the 2nd West Virginia and 14th Pennsylvania Cavalry attacked. The ground over which the 14th Pennsylvania attacked had recently been timbered, and tree trunks and limbs still littered the field, severely impeding their advance.[244] Their charge failed to drive Edgar's determined defenders from their barricade, and the blunted Federals fell back to a grove of sugar maples. Lieutenant Alexander Pentecost, the quartermaster of the 2nd West Virginia, retreated and found himself alone near a maple tree. Pentecost stood there, oblivious to the danger, until some of his comrades called out to him. Pentecost could not make out what they were saying but, on looking at the barricade, figured it out: one of Edgar's men was drawing a bead on him. The Southerner had squeezed off several shots at Pentecost, all of which had missed and caused pieces of bark from the maple tree to fall on the lieutenant. The quartermaster beat a hasty and safe retreat.[245]

The dismounted troopers of the 14th Pennsylvania held the middle of the Federal line. During a full day of stubborn fighting, the Keystone Staters advanced about three hundred yards, but that was it. "The rebel infantry charged the 14th three times with fixed bayonets," remembered the regimental historian, "but the 14th met them and their bayonets with drawn sabers and three times drove them back."[246]

As the guns of both sides belched death, Patton's brigade completed its deployment. Five companies of the 22nd Virginia—Companies A, B, E, G and H—under command of Lieutenant Colonel Andrew R. Barbee, advanced to a fence running across a gentle ascent of open ground, and five more deployed as skirmishers to take possession of a thickly wooded hill to the right of the Miller house, connecting on the right with Edgar's skirmishers. "The skirmishing companies soon became hotly engaged, holding their ground for some time, stubbornly resisting and beating back the enemy until, being attacked by a much superior force, they were compelled to fall back on the line."[247]

The Confederates hastily threw up their crude barricade of fence rails across the road and bottom to a steep, wooded hill on their right where Major Richard Woodram, with three companies of the 26th Virginia, had been posted to observe the enemy's movements in that direction.[248]

"The Federals had a decided advantage in position, and the Confederates were going double-quick…when the Federals reached there and formed their line of battle, protected by the heavy woods and elevations on each side of the ride, and from where they could operate their hidden artillery and infantry and keep under fire the unprotected Confederates, while they were being charged on a down grade by cavalry," recalled a local boy who came

A postwar image of Captain John K. Thompson of the 22nd Virginia Infantry. *Terry Lowry.*

out to witness the spectacle of the battle raging in the valley below. "The Confederates were entirely in the open and without any protection whatever, other than the rail fences…every rail of which showed signs of bullets."[249]

"The enemy began to fire upon us terrifically with his splendid battery, and the increased rattle of musketry, told us that the battle was on," recalled C.W. Humphreys, a member of Edgar's command.

> *Just at this juncture we heard Capt. Thompson in a loud clear voice call out, "Company H, in retreat, march." Then Capt. Read shouted, "Company B, in retreat, march." Springing to my feet I saw that the deep hollow in front of us was occupied by the enemy and were quite close to us. They heard these commands to retreat, and a few of them on horseback dashed up to the opposite side of the fence, and were firing at our retreating men with their pistols.*

Humphreys lost his haversack as he hastily retreated. "Good-bye! I may never need you any how," he thought.[250]

Not long after the 45th Virginia took position behind its portion of the barricade, Colonel Browne got word from Captain Thompson that he was being pressed in front. Browne sent another company to reinforce Thompson under command of Lieutenant Colonel Edwin H. Harman and ordered him to take command of the troops deployed on the ridge. The men of the 45th Virginia could not clearly see the enemy through the thick woods, so they advanced to within fifty yards of Averell's line, "fighting like demons." However, Harman quickly realized that the two companies could not hold the position.[251]

Harman soon afterward reported that a strong force of the enemy was trying to turn the Confederate right. When Browne reported this unwelcome news to Patton, the brigade commander then ordered the entire 45th Virginia to move to the hill to check the flanking movement. Browne deployed his regiment with his right resting on the brow of the first hill at a point opposite the tollgate and his left opposite a point on the road about one hundred yards below the smoldering ruins of the Miller house, facing it.[252] The withdrawal of the 45th Virginia left George Edgar with only four companies to defend the whole line from the mountain on the right to the field occupied by the 22nd Virginia on the left.[253]

Patton sent his adjutant, Lieutenant Noyes Rand of the 22nd Virginia, with an order for Edgar. Rand had to ride diagonally and toward the enemy's fire in order to deliver the message. Just as his horse jumped a low fence, one of Morton's shells burst under the horse, and the poor beast fell on his belly, pitching Rand about ten feet ahead of his head. The shocked adjutant landed on all fours. "I thought of course he was killed outright," recalled Rand, "but as the order was very important, and I found I had no bones broken, I never stopped to even look at my horse but proceeded as fast as I could on foot."

After delivering Patton's order to Colonel Browne, Rand was shocked to find his faithful horse "grazing as if no battle was raging," so he remounted and returned to Patton's command post. "The horse had evidently struck his feet on the top fence rail at the very moment the shell bursted under him, and so gave the tumble. He was unhurt, but strange to say I found on examination several bullets in my saddle—when received God only knows." Rand also discovered that one bullet had passed clear through his uniform vest from side to side and that another had torn the top of his right shoe and then lodged in his wooden stirrup. The ride had been quite the close call indeed.[254]

By the time Browne deployed his troops, Harman had already repulsed Averell's initial attack and then had dealt with a determined assault on the left of the 45th Virginia's line. Browne had left Major Alexander M. Davis in charge of the center of his line, and Davis ordered a company forward to support Harman's left wing. This movement drove back Averell's attackers, and Davis advanced his company about one hundred yards beyond and perpendicular to the line of his left wing. Browne also sent two of his companies to reinforce Woodram's position on the ridge.[255]

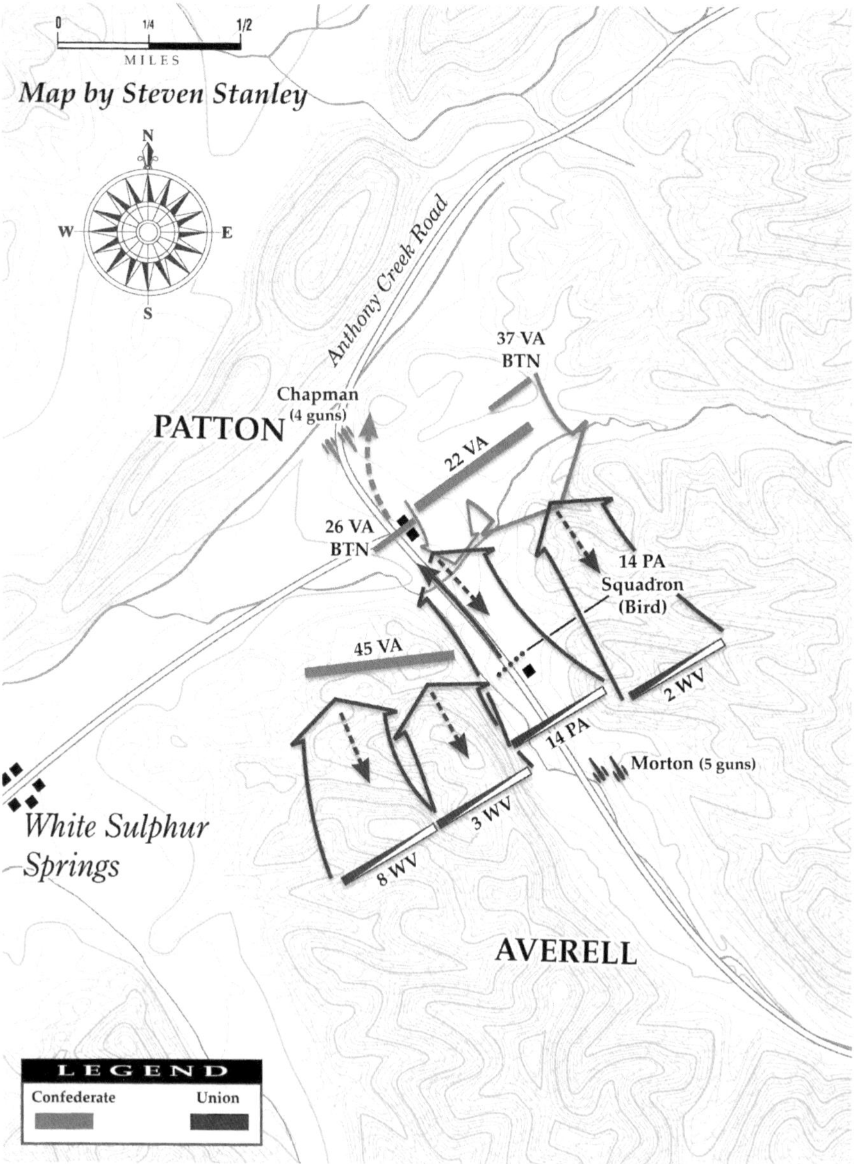

The battle rages, afternoon, August 26, 1863.

The Union troops pressed their attack, driving back the two companies of skirmishers. "It was a veritable battle-storm for about fifteen minutes, when the enemy retreated, leaving some of their dead close to our line of battle," continued Humphreys. "A few of the left companies of the 22nd broke to the rear, but seeing that the rest stood their ground, and meeting Derrick's Battalion just at the right time arriving on the line of battle, they returned and fought it out there. Edgar's men stood to their work splendidly. The enemy were repulsed but not whipped."[256] One observer noted, "The Yankees would have come out victorious if [Derrick's Battalion] hadn't got there when they did."[257]

Morton advanced his surviving guns to within six hundred yards of the Confederate barricade, where they opened on Chapman's gunners and on the Southern infantrymen. Chapman's guns responded "with great spirit and accuracy," and "an artillery duel of great heat ensued and lasted for more than two hours, when one of our pieces was disabled and another temporarily silenced," as Patton described the counter-battery duel that broke out.[258]

"If there was ever such a thing as an artillery duel fought, it was done right there," recalled one of Chapman's gunners. "Averell had four guns, we the same number, and were only a few hundred yards apart, and in full view; each was a target for the other, and for the space of several hours we exchanged shots as fast as it was possible to do…The Federals surely had expert gunners."[259]

Sergeant H.A. Evans commanded one of Morton's guns. During the savage counter-battery duel, Evans was struck on the right side of the head by a piece of shell that exploded just over his head and was only saved by the shrapnel being deflected by striking the band of his hat. "He was knocked senseless and the bone badly shattered," recorded his unit's historian in 1890, "seventeen pieces being taken out and it now troubles him severely."[260]

"It affords me great pleasure to bear testimony to the

A postwar image of Major William L. McLaughlin, chief of artillery for Sam Jones's Department. *Robert Driver.*

efficiency with which the battery was handled, and to its marked effect upon the enemy, as attested to by the destruction of the timber in and around [Ewing's] battery, and by one of his guns being permanently disabled and another dismounted, the carriage of which was left upon the field," wrote an admiring Major William McLaughlin, the chief of artillery for the Department of Western Virginia. "The men of the battery stood bravely and steadily by their guns, though subjected to a steady, hot, and well-directed fire from the enemy's guns, and too much credit cannot be afforded to Captain Chapman for the zeal, gallantry, and energy displayed by him throughout the engagement."[261]

In ordering an advance of his whole line, Averell sent von König with the left wing, consisting of the 2nd and 8th West Virginia, forward, and he also ordered his right wing to advance. He deployed Gibson's battalion around the Miller house and outbuildings, which sat in front of the Confederate center. "The enemy clung tenaciously to the wooded hill to their right, and Gibson's battalion was driven from the house by a regiment of the enemy which at the moment arrived upon the field," recounted Averell. The Union general immediately had the house set ablaze by artillery shells, preventing the Confederates from using it as a sniper's den.[262]

Lieutenant J. Calvin French of the 2nd West Virginia had command of a portion of his regiment's skirmish line, which was in advance of Morton's guns. While leading his troops, French received a severe wound near his right knee that distorted the joint and caused him pain for the rest of his life. His comrades rescued him and brought him back to safety before he fell into the hands of the enemy. His battle was over.[263]

"The action became general and heavy," reported Patton.

> *Our skirmishers in advance on the left were now hotly pressed by largely superior numbers, but under the leadership of Lieut. Col. Andrew R. Barbee, of the Twenty-second Virginia Regiment, held their ground with admirable tenacity until their ammunition was exhausted, when they fell back in good order without any confusion, and, with the exception of a part of one company which was able to rejoin its regiment, were, by the nature of the ground, forced to take position on the extreme left of our line.*

Barbee was severely wounded in the arm during this movement and was then beaten in the hip with the butt of a Federal carbine while he lay on the ground.[264]

The men of the 22nd Virginia faced an extremely difficult situation. They held a spot out in the open without even so much as a low rail fence to protect them. The Virginians were exposed to heavy fire of musketry as well as blasts of grapeshot, shell and canister from Morton's guns, "which the enemy threw with great accuracy."[265] Major Robert Augustus Bailey, who succeeded Barbee in command of the 22nd Virginia, had nothing but praise for his soldiers. "Notwithstanding the great disadvantages under which they labored, the officers and men acted most nobly, repelling the oft-repeated and daring attempts of the enemy to dislodge them," he wrote. "The commanders of companies and their subaltern officers are entitled to much praise for their coolness under fire and the tenacity with which they held their ground."[266]

The fierce struggle between the 8th West Virginia and the 22nd Virginia hid an especially poignant story. "In the encounter between the 8th and the [Rebel] 22nd, there was something terrible, for it was really a conflict between brothers, cousins, and neighbor boys, for these two regiments were made up in the same section of country in West Virginia," observed a captain of the 8th West Virginia.[267]

Thirty-one-year-old Lieutenant John Gay Carr of the 22nd Virginia, known to his friends as Gay, a native of Charleston, had served in Colonel Patton's militia company, the Kanawha Riflemen. Carr was known as a promising young man who had exhibited the noblest qualities of a soldier both in the ranks and as an officer. "Lieutenant Gay Carr, of the Kanawha Riflemen fell with a bullet through his brain," recounted Rand. He died on the field.[268] The popular officer was buried in the Old Stone Church Cemetery in nearby Lewisburg, and his friends and comrades later raised money to erect a handsome tree trunk monument over his grave in 1904.[269]

Averell's dismounted horse soldiers made repeated charges on both the right and the left of the Confederate line, which Patton's determined defenders repulsed again and again. On the right, Baron von König and his two regiments were only able to advance a short distance through protracted, hard fighting. "Desperate efforts were made to dislodge the Forty-fifth Regiment, but the steadiness of that regiment and the courage and skill of its commander foiled them all," reported George Patton.[270]

"From the position of our battery, we could only tell what was going on by the noise," recalled one of Chapman's gunners. "Our men said the Federals would come within twenty or thirty yards of them, and then there was a

Captain Robert H. Hubble, Major William Blessing and Captain John T. Kincannon, 23rd Battalion Virginia Infantry. *Smith County Historical Society Museum.*

tremendous roar of musketry for a few minutes, which was always followed by the 'rebel yell' by which we knew the results."[271]

As more and more of Averell's troopers engaged, Patton grew worried that he had sufficient troops to withstand the onslaught. Luckily, he received reinforcements at the right moment. As noted earlier, Lieutenant Colonel Clarence Derrick and his 23rd Virginia Battalion, accompanied by about two hundred troopers of the 37th Battalion of Virginia Cavalry, arrived from guarding the Greenbrier Bridge. "We were roused up and hastily retraced our journey to the Dolan place, where we paused about an hour, and then pushed on rapidly to the junction of the Anthony's Creek road with the James and Kanawha turnpike, where Henry Miller had a store," recounted one of Derrick's officers.[272]

Derrick and his battalion immediately advanced to the left of the 22nd Virginia, first extending the Confederate line of battle. However, Derrick determined that the position could not be held, so he positioned his men some one hundred yards to the rear of the left of the line in a position that could not be outflanked to the left by Averell's men.[273]

In order to reach his position, Derrick and his men were "compelled to move under a perfect storm of shot and shell, which caused some loss and some confusion, which latter was quickly remedied by that gallant officer." Patton directed two of Derrick's companies, under command of Major

William Blessing, to advance across the open field under heavy fire and took position on the left of the 22nd Virginia, extending the Confederate line of battle.[274] "These companies, led by Major Blessing, gallantly charged to the position assigned them through a perfect storm of shot, shell, and ball," wrote Derrick in praise of his subordinate.[275]

Patton's infantrymen stood firm. "Our infantry, when they got into line, were like a Stonewall, and held their position from start to finish," remembered one of Chapman's artillerists. "In front of them the woods were dense with an undergrowth of bushes, except in the center where the men had no protection save an old rail fence." These men were fighting to defend their homes and families, and they fought "like tigers, and every man of our forces acted the hero; hence any one arrogating for himself special heroism is an egotist and unworthy of credence," he sniffed.[276] An eyewitness later said that the road "was strewn with dead and wounded soldiers."[277]

About this time, Chapman's guns ran low on ammunition. Captain Chapman told Sergeant John G. Stevens to take two limbers and go to the caissons, parked a short distance away, for a fresh supply. When he returned with the fresh ammunition, Stevens learned that Chapman had withdrawn the guns about two hundred yards to the rear. "I never knew why he did that unless it was for protection while they were not in action, and waiting for a supply of ammunition," remembered Stevens.[278]

"It then became an affair of sharpshooters along the whole line at a distance of less than 100 yards," reported Averell. "The effort which my men had made in scaling a succession of heights on either hand had wearied them almost to exhaustion. A careful fire was kept up by small arms fire for three hours, it being almost impossible for either side to advance or retire."

Two soldiers of the 22nd Virginia distinguished themselves during this phase of the battle. Albert Singleton of Company H and another soldier identified only as "Huffman" were on the 22nd Virginia's skirmish line, behind trees. Singleton occasionally stepped out from behind the trees and drew enemy fire. Huffman, who was a crack shot, darted out from behind his tree and picked off the Yankee horse soldiers who had fired at Singleton. When a friend asked Singleton why he took such a risk, Singleton responded, "The Yankees couldn't shoot."[279]

While this heavy firing continued, the fearless New York general reconnoitered his entire position, going from the hills on the left to the right, looking for a place to probe Patton's line for weaknesses to exploit.[280]

The day's drama was about to reach its climax.

5

Costly Climax on August 26

About four o'clock on the warm, sunny afternoon of August 26, 1863, Union commander Brigadier General William Woods Averell decided to make an all-out effort to dislodge Patton's Confederates from their strong position blocking the New Yorker's route of march to his target in Lewisburg. He sent for Captain John Bird's squadron of about one hundred troopers of the 14th Pennsylvania Cavalry, which had not been dismounted during the earlier fighting, and ordered them to make a mounted charge against the Southern barricade. Averell sent instructions to his commanders along the line that he was about to unleash a cavalry charge on the enemy's center and ordered them to act in concert with that mounted attack. Captain Bird ordered his men to draw sabers, put their spurs to their horses and charge.[281]

The Pennsylvanians thundered toward Edgar's position behind the barricade, their sabers glinting in the afternoon sunlight, making what Edgar described as a "furious charge."[282] The sight impressed the other Union horse soldiers. The regimental historian of the 2nd West Virginia declared:

> *This brave body of men made one of the most daring charges of the war, not only facing a murderous storm of leaden hail from the front but also, to their surprise, received an enfilading fire along their flank from a large body of infantry concealed in a cornfield to the left of the road. On they dashed, regardless of death and danger, and reached the breastworks of felled trees and fence rails thrown across the road.*[283]

Seeing the mounted charge bearing down on them, about three hundred Confederates abandoned the barricade, running for their lives. Schoonmaker's troopers opened on the fleeing Southerners, inflicting heavy casualties on them. Reserves came up to shove back the mounted Yankees, and Patton's men soon regained control of the barricade.[284] Bird was badly wounded during the attack and was captured.[285] Patton claimed that the Pennsylvanians were "driven back in utter confusion and rout, many of their horses coming into our lines."[286] Lieutenant Colonel Edgar later claimed that "not more than five of the enemy" returned in their saddles.[287]

The rest of the 14th Pennsylvania Cavalry then received orders to make a mounted attack in the wake of Bird's repulse. The Pennsylvanians charged "through a ravine in the face of a galling front fire, almost up to the enemy's fortifications, exposed to a withering enfilade fire, but the Pennsylvanians—'the charging regiment'—rode on, and on, into the very jaws of death with artillery and infantry pouring deadly missiles into its ranks—till it reached the enemy's breastworks, and got tangled up with the abatis the enemy had placed in front of their fortifications where many of our boys were killed, wounded, or captured," the regimental historian of the 14th Pennsylvania Cavalry colorfully reported.[288] After firing a volley, and without time to reload, Patton's infantrymen clubbed their muskets to knock the Northern horse soldiers from their mounts and then pulled the dazed cavalrymen over the barricade and made them prisoners.[289]

Colonel James M. Schoonmaker had his horse shot out from under him and fell beside a dead Union officer. Major General Sam Jones recognized Schoonmaker's horse, saddle and bridle after the battle and reported the colonel's death to Richmond in his after-action report of the battle. However, Schoonmaker was unhurt; he immediately mounted the dead officer's horse and safely led his men back from the barricade. Lieutenant Jacob Shoop of Company M was badly wounded in the thigh during the charge.[290]

Private Adolphus Meeker had enlisted in Company L of the 14th Pennsylvania Cavalry on September 20, 1862, at the tender age of fifteen. He was the youngest of five brothers to serve in the Union army during the Civil War. He had served with the regiment since its early days, and he was in the saddle when the Pennsylvanians made their mounted charge that afternoon. Meeker was killed that afternoon at the age of seventeen while making the brave charge against the barricade. Another of his brothers died in July 1864 at the notorious Confederate prisoner-of-war camp at Andersonville.[291]

Sergeant John Stevens of Chapman's Battery had a clear view of the dramatic charge. Stevens was filling several canteens for the battery's wounded men when he spotted the charging Pennsylvanians. "I saw the company being formed on the pike by fours, and start with a whoop down the road, with drawn sabers, coming in a lope, four in a breast," he wrote.

> *The lay of the land was such that I could not see our men, and the thought struck me that our men were retreating and gone and here I am looking right into the door of "Camp Chase." I didn't know if I could have run if I had tried to. I always dreaded being captured, but I soon got relief. Edgar's men had built a high fence across the pike in front of them, and the head of the column of cavalry came right up to the fence, when Edgar's men fired on them, with a tremendous volley which gave me instant relief. Horses reared and fell, and such a mix-up I never saw before. The men that escaped wheeled and went back like they were racing, several horses going without riders.*[292]

Stevens and his comrades captured one of the Pennsylvanians. Stevens asked, "Why did you make that fool charge?" The Keystone Stater responded, "The General said to our Colonel, 'Can't you take your men and go down there and take those fellows?' I thought the whole regiment was coming, but when I looked back I saw it was only one company."[293] The 14th Pennsylvania Cavalry lost 103 men in the day's brutal fighting.[294]

Corporal Charles A. Mestrezat served in Company E of the 14th Pennsylvania. "We had a very hard fight the 26th of August," he told his wife. "Many of our boys were killed & wounded. I, through God's kind providence escaped unhurt though much exposed. I feel truly thankful to God for his protection in the hour of danger; before I went into the fight I put my trust in him." However, Mestrezat was captured during the charge on the barricade. "I have been very kindly treated as well as the rest of the prisoners. I could not be better treated anywhere than I am here. The citizens & soldiers do all they can for our wounded, in truth they are just as kind a people as can be found either inside or outside our lines." Within a few days, he was confined on overcrowded Belle Isle in Richmond, a filthy and terrible prison camp. Mestrezat never returned from Belle Isle. He died there on March 7, 1864.[295]

Lieutenant Colonel Edgar of the 26th Battalion of Virginia Infantry disputed the Federal claims that the charge of the 14th Pennsylvania Cavalry reached the barricade. "The road along which the charge was made was blockaded within fifty yards of the stockade (or barricade) by the dead and wounded bodies of the men and horses of the splendid regiment, and not more than five of the troopers returned in their saddles," he declared.[296]

Another officer of the 14th Pennsylvania drew Averell's ire during this attack. Captain Robert Pollock of the 14th Pennsylvania "failed to make his appearance within view of the enemy, and remained behind in a secluded place, with most of his company, where, I am informed, he was found asleep by the enemy after the command had been withdrawn."[297] Given that, Pollock probably deserved to be captured.

During this attack, the fearless Baron Paul von König, who had earned a well-deserved reputation as Averell's most daring scout, led a portion of the 14th Pennsylvania's attack on the right. Baron von König was ordered to clear out of a white frame house Confederate sharpshooters who were sniping away at Morton's gunners and inflicting losses on them from the safety of the house. One of Morton's gunners set the house ablaze with an artillery shell, and von König led the dismounted Pennsylvania horse soldiers in an attack on the Confederates who had vacated the house.[298] One of Patton's foot soldiers drew a bead on the mounted German officer with the long, flowing hair, and von König dropped from the saddle, killed instantly, shot in the back. He was buried beneath a tree below the road near the spot where he fell.[299]

Averell also ordered the officers commanding the regiments on the right to press forward at the same time as the mounted charge to try to push their way through to the Anthony's Creek road, which came in on the Confederate left. Lieutenant John Combs, the regimental adjutant of the 2nd West Virginia, failed to find Colonel George R. Latham, the colonel of the 2nd West Virginia, in time, so he delivered Averell's order to the portion of the regiment nearest to him. That meant that only part of the 2nd West Virginia received the order to attack.[300] In the meantime, Lieutenant Morton changed front and raked the Confederate line in the cornfield with canister from his four guns, "causing the enemy who were massed there, a greater loss in men than from any other source during the battle."[301]

Major Patrick McNally, who commanded the right battalion of the 2nd West Virginia, joined with Lieutenant Combs to lead the 2nd West Virginia forward against the portion of the barricade held by the 22nd Virginia. McNally, age thirty, was an Irish immigrant who had previously served in the U.S. Navy. He settled in Ironton, Ohio, and personally raised the first company that left Ironton for service in the Civil War, Company K of what became the 2nd West Virginia.[302] With only about one hundred men, the attack led by McNally—"foremost in the line, waving his sword and cheering his men"—and Combs advanced on the enemy barricade and drove its defenders away in what Patton described as a "determined charge" that was "handsomely repulsed."[303]

Major Patrick McNally, 2nd West Virginia Mounted Infantry, was mortally wounded during the afternoon attack on the barricade. *Frank S. Reader,* History of the Fifth West Virginia Cavalry.

"We advanced through the cornfield, meeting with a murderous fire from the enemy, safely posted behind their breastworks," remembered a member of the 2nd West Virginia. "We pressed onward, however, almost up to the fortifications, but were there met with such a withering fire that human endurance could stand it no longer, and we fell back a short distance, taking position in a gully or dry creek bed, where we were partially sheltered. In that severe charge some of our bravest officers and men fell."[304]

The rest of the regiment failed to support McNally's attack, which was forced back by a vicious counterattack by the 22nd Virginia and two companies of Derrick's Battalion, commanded by Major William Blessing, that came to the aid of the hard-pressed 22nd Virginia.[305] McNally grabbed hold of a Confederate at the barricade and captured him, but the Irish major was mortally wounded and taken prisoner by the Confederates.[306] Six of Averell's men dashed forward to try to rescue McNally, but all were captured, ending any further attempts to rescue the fallen major, who was left to his unhappy fate.[307] Patton later reported that his defenders killed and wounded many of the West Virginians within "15 paces of our lines."[308]

Henry C. Carpenter, one of Patton's foot soldiers, had a clear view of McNally's wounding and capture. His poor spelling, grammar and punctuation are presented here just as he originally wrote his letter:

> *One of the charges was they made on us was led by a Magor the Magor himself succeeded in getting through our lines he ran and squatted down behind a stump then jumpted up and drawd his sword on one of our men and demanded him to surrender which the fellow did the Magor taken him by the Collar and started back to the yankey lines when some of our men noticed him going back and shot him down and wonded the prisoner he had taken.*[309]

Major Augustus Bailey, who succeeded the wounded Lieutenant Colonel Barbee in command of the 22nd Virginia, described this as a "spirited and bold charge" upon his lines. "This may be considered the most critical moment," recounted Bailey.

> *My ammunition was almost entirely exhausted—few had more than five rounds, many none at all. This caused some to break to the rear, but they were easily rallied by their company officers. The enemy, advancing with loud cheers, made a most desperate assault on our lines. Here the bravery of the troops was conspicuous. Led on by their company officers, they determinedly met the foe and repulsed them in handsome style, driving them in confusion beyond their own lines, killing many, and wounding and capturing the field-officer* [McNally] *who headed the charge.*[310]

Patton realized, "Having thus tried the left and center [and failed], a very heavy force of at least two regiments was formed to force my right, but Colonel Browne, ever vigilant, informed me in time to send him Major [James R.] Claiborne, with about 200 men of the Thirty-seventh Battalion [of Virginia Cavalry], and with them again repulsed the enemy with great slaughter."[311]

The 45th Virginia repulsed multiple attacks in its front. "After they had charged our regt. Four different times—and had been repulsed—the next time they came through the brush and go up to within 20 paces before we saw them—and the officers halloed to us—damn you—ain't you Rebles going to run," recounted Lieutenant Colonel Edwin Harman of the 45th Virginia. "One my fellows—replied—no damn you we aint and then we gave them such a terrific fire they could not withstand it and ran themselves."[312]

Colonel William H. Browne of the 45th Virginia realized that Averell was getting ready to attack again. He brought his reserve battalion forward just in time to help repulse "two furious attacks of the enemy re-enforced."[313] As Lieutenant Colonel Harman proudly declared, "Our regt. repulsed eight heavy and furious charges."[314]

The 3rd and 8th West Virginia also met a superior force of the enemy posted in their front and failed to dislodge it after a desperate struggle.[315] Lieutenant Colonel Francis Thompson, the commander of the 3rd West Virginia, made himself conspicuous with his cool courage under fire. He "stood in the hottest of the fire, leading his brave men not less than seven times in desperate charges upon the enemy. They lying in ambush our men would move upon them under any disadvantage, though thus to move was almost certain destruction," remembered one of Thompson's troopers. "Yet as one order would come after another from the General, to charge on the enemy, the Colonel, cool and brave, would again and again renew the charge. Here more men were killed than anywhere else on the field."[316]

"It was now getting late in the evening," reported George Patton. "The enemy had been repulsed at all points, and not a foot of ground lost by our men since morning. For some time the action was almost suspended, except for the dropping fire of sharpshooters and the occasional boom of a gun."[317] At dusk, though, Morton's guns opened again with a fresh fury, foretelling yet another impending attack. Averell ordered a final mounted attack against Edgar's Battalion in the center by the men who had spent the day holding the horses of the dismounted soldiers on the firing line. These men made a mounted charge down a narrow road enclosed on both sides by high, stout post and rail fences. Edgar's men held their fire until the charge was within just a few yards—Edgar later estimated that they came within fifty yards—of the barricade and then unloosed a savage volley into their faces, halting the charge in its tracks.[318] Chapman's weary artillerists helped to repulse the last-ditch Union attack, the "guns speaking in tongues of flame and tones of thunder in the gathering darkness," as one early historian put it.[319]

Edgar's soldiers poured volley after volley into the struggling mass of blue-clad horsemen, and dead men and horses littered the road. Dead horses blocked the route of retreat of the Federal cavalry, meaning that "it was fearful to see how they were butchered and shot, and all, as I say, just for nothing," noted a member of the 14th Pennsylvania Cavalry.[320] Finally, after nine hours of heavy fighting, the firing sputtered out.

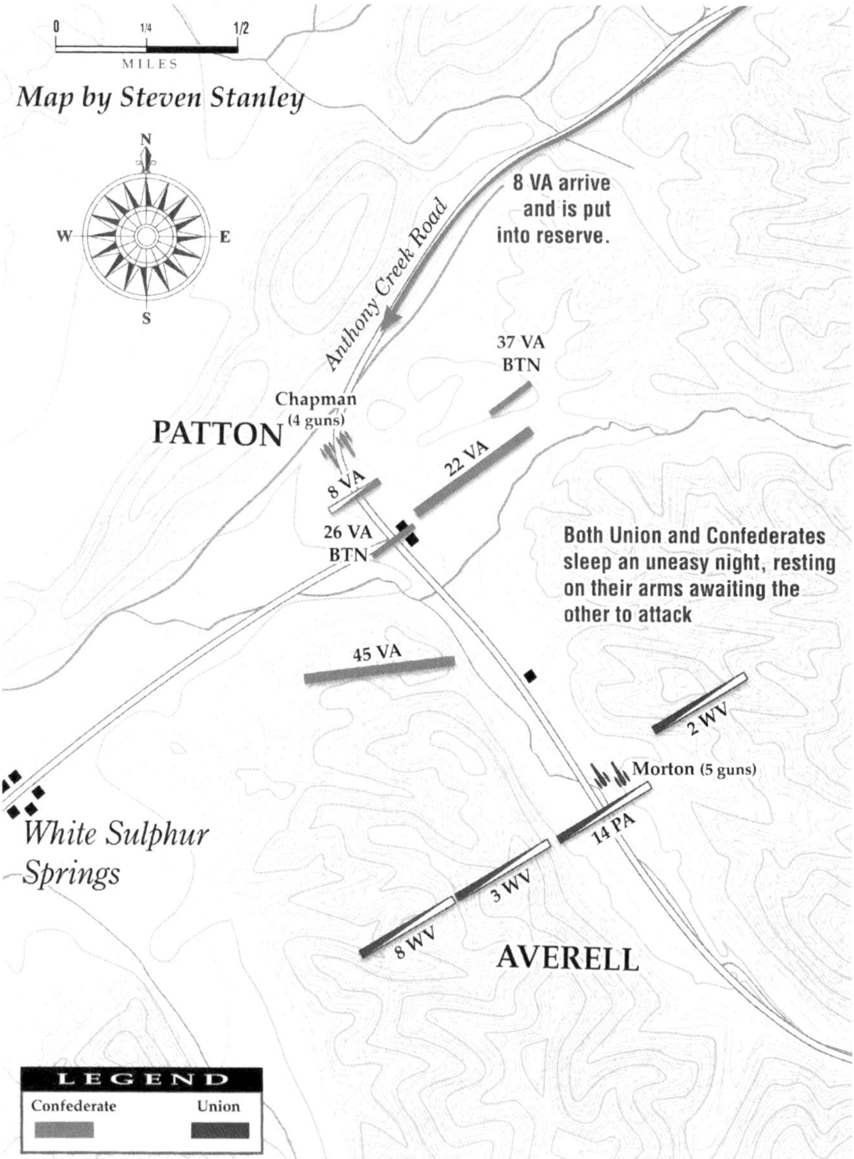

The situation at the end of the day on August 26, 1863.

"The battle was sanguinary considering the numbers engaged," reported a member of the 8th West Virginia, "and having the advantage of position, the rebels fought desperately."[321] A trooper of the 3rd West Virginia recounted, "It is generally conceded that all the regiments fought desperately. Officers and soldiers showed an unyielding purpose to fight until the enemy was routed."[322] A Confederate sounded a more colorful note: "The battle raged with a fury equaled only by the hate of the War Gods, the entire day and part of the night."[323]

Averell's all-out attack had failed, and he soon began receiving reports that his entire command was running very short on ammunition. Although Averell did not know it, Patton faced the same problem. "The slackened fire of the enemy evidently indicated that his supply was not plentiful," noted Averell, as the intensity of the daylong, severe fighting finally petered out.[324] It was now dark, and the two armies lay in the same positions they had held all day. Both sides posted sentries in front of their lines, and both sides lay down to rest less than three hundred yards apart.[325]

Colonel John H. Oley of the 8th West Virginia had shifted his command late in the afternoon. Five of his companies linked up with the far end of Latham's 3rd West Virginia. Another company was sent to the center to support Morton's guns, and yet another company went to guard Averell's wagon train and serve as a rear guard.[326] An officer of the 8th West Virginia left a detailed description of the horror of that night. "Our boys held the positions that they took and lay on their arms all night without food, fire or blankets, with the pickets of each side less than fifty yards from each other, expecting to renew the battle with the dawn," he reported. "I will not attempt to describe our feelings during the fearful night. Surrounded with the dead, for the rebel dead were within our own lines. Our dead had been removed, and our wounded cared for."[327]

"The boys on the firing line were greatly exhausted not having had anything to eat or drink since the beginning of the battle, the morning before," recalled a member of the 14th Pennsylvania. The horse holders, who had not been involved in the day's fighting, lit fires and cooked coffee, which, along with some hardtack, was brought to the men on the front lines in the hope of making their plight a little less unpleasant.[328]

"During that long night, the enemy attempted to surprise and capture us," noted an officer of the 14th Pennsylvania Cavalry, "but we slept on our arms in line of battle—if we slept at all—and were ready for the onslaught. It was made with great loss of life on both sides."[329] Firing continued at intervals during the night, with the opposing forces popping away at each other at short range, their muzzle flashes lighting up the inky darkness of the late August night.[330] One soldier of Chapman's battery remembered that Averell's determined horse soldiers "charged all night from 1 to 2 hours apart. The last charge just before day was the most determined and the hardest to repel."[331] There is no record of there being so many charges once the sun went down, but this account illustrates the stress faced by Patton's soldiers that warm night.

All day, Averell had expected to hear that infantry reinforcements from the Kanawha Division, part of Brigadier General Eliakim P. Scammon's Subdistrict of the Kanawha, who were expected to be coming from the west to meet Averell's command, would soon link up with his tired horse soldiers. However, no word came from Scammon's troops, and Averell slowly came to the realization that he would have to stand pat with the forces that he had available. Averell had all of his remaining supply of ammunition brought up from the brigade's wagon train, and he deployed every available man on the line of battle.[332] However, that meant that Averell had no hope of resupplying his horse soldiers if their meager supply of ammunition ran out. They would not have sufficient ammunition to carry on the fight for long the next day if the battle resumed with the ferocity that had marked the first day's combat.

Both commanders held councils of war with their subordinates that night. Averell conducted his at about 11:00 p.m. and inquired of his officers whether they should stay and fight or withdraw. All of his subordinates favored withdrawal, but the New Yorker stubbornly refused, preferring to stay and fight, and he assumed all responsibility for the outcome. Patton also met with his subordinates at about the same time. Most, if not all, of the Confederate subordinate commanders preferred a retreat to at least a more favorable position, if not altogether, but Patton told them that he would not do so. He declared that he would assume all responsibility for the outcome and continue the fight, even if it cost his entire command. Thus, with the fateful decision by both commanders to stay and fight, the die was cast for the next day's action.[333]

Averell understood that he had to make a difficult decision. "It was quite evident to my mind that if the resistance of the enemy was kept up, I could go no farther in that direction," he wrote. "It was impossible to retire during the night without disorder and perhaps disaster. By remaining until morning two chances remained with me: first, the enemy might retreat, and, second, Scammon might arrive." Left with no option, the New Yorker decided to wait out a long and unpleasant night on the battlefield, just a few hundred yards from the enemy's lines. In the meantime, he made every arrangement possible for a speedy withdrawal the next day if necessary.[334] "Our company was on picket and we could hear the rebels talking and preparing to resume the struggle the next day," remembered Sergeant Jacob Groft of Company M of the 14th Pennsylvania Cavalry.[335]

Colonel George S. Patton spent the long night bristling with nervous energy. He visited his lines, strengthened his weak points and tended to the wounded, who were removed from the battlefield to receive medical care. "During the night the command was busily engaged preparing for the following day," noted the commander of Patton's 22nd Virginia.[336] Patton extended his line farther to the right by putting the entire 45th Virginia on the line of battle while Edgar's men bolstered the barricade they had constructed that morning.[337] About 2:00 a.m. on the twenty-seventh, Patton also received reinforcements in the form of five companies of Colonel James M. Corns's 8th Virginia Cavalry.[338] Patton dismounted the weary troopers of the 8th Virginia and placed two companies of them, under the command of Major Thomas P. Bowen, in reserve immediately in rear of Edgar's Battalion, which held the center of the Confederate line.[339]

Colonel James M. Corns, commander of the 8th Virginia Cavalry. *Judy R. West.*

Dr. John A. Hunter, the Confederate medical director, designated the world-famous White Hotel, Greenbrier Resort, as a field infirmary for those wounded in the Battle of White Sulphur Springs. While the battle raged on August 26, George Patton's wife, Sue, and their three children were a scant three miles away, occupying a cabin at the Greenbrier. Sue Patton heard the guns barking all day, and when battle casualties were brought to the Greenbrier for medical care, she rolled up her sleeves and helped to tend to the wounded. Patton's seven-year-old son George William joined in, "following my mother around with a bucket and sponge. The smell was so awful that my mother fainted and had to be carried out." Colonel Patton himself didn't get over to the Greenbrier to see his family until August 28, and when he did make his way there, he was so

Brigadier General Gabriel Wharton, who commanded another of Jones's infantry brigades. Blue & Gray *magazine*.

dirty and bedraggled that George William did not recognize him right away.[340]

Major General Sam Jones was worried and had been for several days. He did not believe that Patton's single brigade would be able to stop Averell's raid if the New Yorker received reinforcements from Scammon's command. Jones called out the Home Guard—mostly composed of men over the conscription age of forty-five—to protect the New River Bridge and the Virginia Central Railroad.[341] Although he had asked Confederate secretary of war James Seddon to send him the brigades of Brigadier General Albert G. Jenkins and Brigadier General Gabriel Wharton, which had been detached from Jones's department and sent to the Army of Northern Virginia, on August 24, he repeated that request. Although Jones ordered the two brigades to return by way of Staunton and Warm Springs, they did not arrive in time to make a difference, which only added to Jones's rising level of concern that his available forces would not be able to prevent Averell from breaking through Patton's roadblock.[342]

Colonel William L. "Mudwall" Jackson had ordered Major Joseph K. Kesler to take a detachment of the 19th Virginia Cavalry to Covington and, if possible, to Lewisburg to ascertain and report the movements of Averell's force. The 20th Virginia Cavalry, another portion of Jackson's command, under command of Colonel William W. Arnett, arrived at Warm Springs and reported that Averell had moved on from Warm Springs and that the enemy's infantry had fallen back to the Gatewood Plantation in Pocahontas County. Jackson ordered Arnett to scout after the enemy in the hope of learning more that would enable them to interdict Averell's command and gain some revenge for the humiliation they had received at Huntersville a few days earlier.[343]

Patton and his weary Southern infantrymen hunkered down behind their barricade and waited to see whether Averell would renew the attack in the morning.

6

Averell Withdraws

Averell hoped that by waiting, either he would receive reinforcements and a fresh supply of ammunition or Patton would retreat. With the coming of dawn, Averell discovered not only that Patton's stubborn infantrymen were still there but also that they had received reinforcements in the form of Corns's five companies of cavalrymen. He heard no word from Scammon and realized that he had no choice but to withdraw. Averell made detailed arrangements to make a prompt withdrawal from the battlefield in the face of the enemy. "The ambulances loaded with wounded, the caissons, wagons and long columns of horses were placed in proper order upon the road, details made for the attendance of the wounded, trees prepared to fell across the gorge when our artillery should have passed, and commanding officers received their instructions," Averell wrote in his after-action report.[344]

William Woods Averell was a very intelligent man, and he had learned from his prior experiences. On March 17, 1863, his Second Cavalry Division of the Army of the Potomac's Cavalry Corps had fought the Battle of Kelly's Ford. The Confederate defenders delayed the Union advance for nearly three hours by felling trees across the road, forcing Averell to bring up axmen to clear the abatis created by the felled trees. The delay bought sufficient time for the cavalry brigade of Brigadier General Fitzhugh Lee and a battery of Confederate horse artillery to reach the battlefield at Kelly's Ford. The delay engendered by the felling of those trees cost Averell the initiative in the battle and greatly frustrated his efforts to reach Culpeper.[345]

The painful lesson taught by that frustrating experience still stung the New Yorker, and he decided to use the same tactic on Patton's infantrymen and his small force of cavalry. He hoped it would be as successful as the Confederate use of that tactic had been at Kelly's Ford five months earlier.

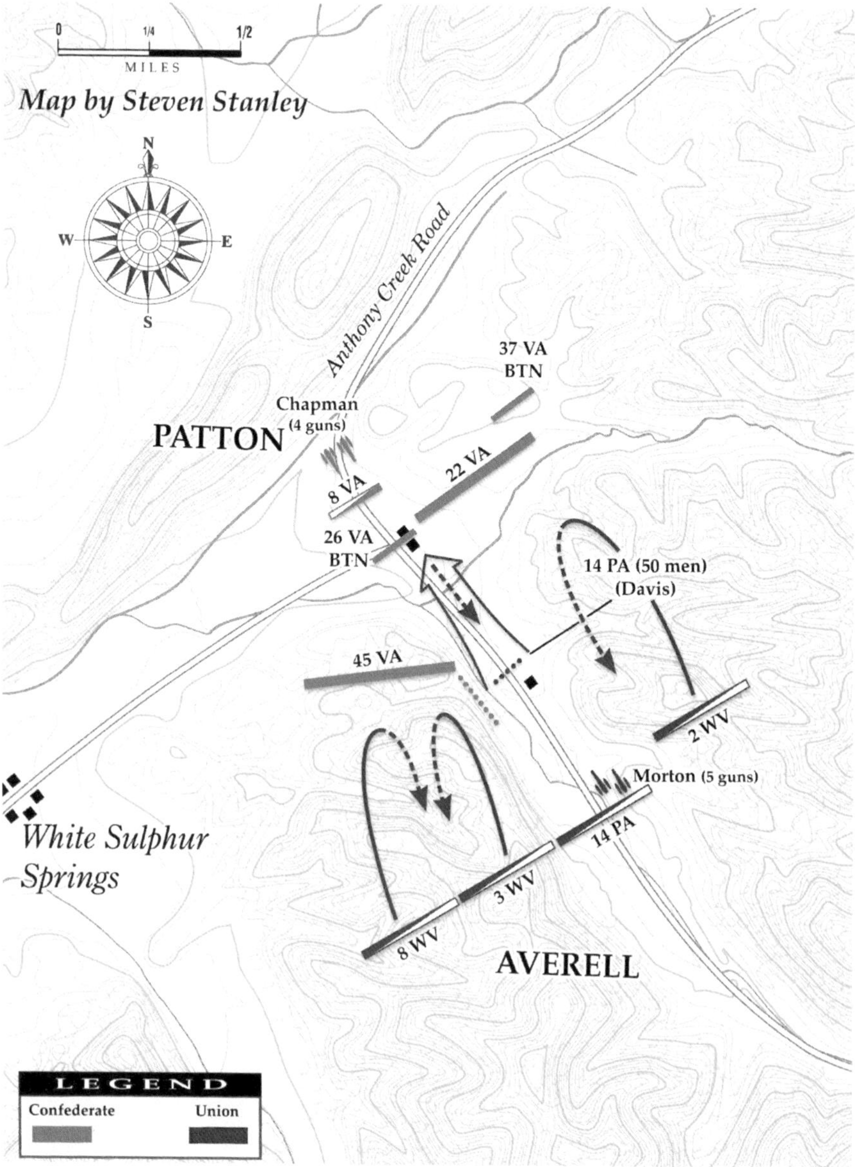

Day two of the battle, August 27, 1863.

Averell had his pioneers partially chop down the largest trees during the night so that they were ready to fall across the gorge and block the pursuit of the enemy with just a few more whacks of an axe. The plan worked to perfection. "As soon as we had passed the gorge, the trees went crashing down completely obstructing it," recorded an officer of the 2nd West Virginia.[346]

Early on the morning of August 27, Major General Sam Jones, Patton's commander, reported to the Confederate War Department. "Some desultory firing this morning early, and expect the fight to be renewed any minute."[347] He was right—Averell intended to make a final attempt to break through Patton's line. "At daybreak the attempt was again made to storm our position," reported Patton, "but with so little spirit that it was evident that the enemy had lost confidence."

Averell's troopers advanced at about five o'clock that morning and drove in Lieutenant Colonel Edgar's pickets. A "desultory fire was kept up between our sharpshooters and those of the enemy until about 11 a.m.," reported Edgar, "at which time a spirited fire was commenced, which was continued until the enemy retired."[348]

Averell called for fifty volunteers to make a mounted charge on the barricade. Corporal William A.R. Davis of Company G of the 14th Pennsylvania answered the call. "We had to charge by fours," he recalled, "so when we got there, not a man was left on horseback but Sgt. McCay, who wheeled his horse and got back." Averell ordered these men to dismount and use their carbines if they could not break through the barricade. "I was left there with only one man," recalled Davis, "and he could not fire his carbine for he was wounded and dying, with his back against the barricade." Davis left him there and headed off alone on foot until he spotted the rest of the brigade's dismounted men, all of whom had had their horses shot out from under them all along the road on the way to the barricade. "There must have been some unseen hand that protected me through that storm of lead," recalled a relieved Davis. He jumped in between two logs that lay on the side of the road, landing among other troopers of his regiment. They remained there, exposed to fire from both sides, for nearly two hours before making a mad dash to safety. "If I had stayed at the barricade I would be dead and buried away down in Dixie now," concluded Davis.[349]

Colonel William H. Browne's 45th Virginia faced only one attack on the morning of August 27, so Browne deployed a line of skirmishers from his left wing along the ridge line, enabling his men to maintain a cross-fire to the position held by Edgar's Battalion, meaning that the Confederates laid down a deadly fire that discouraged further attacks by Averell's horse soldiers.[350] Chapman's guns opened again, and Morton's guns replied, and the prior day's vicious counter-battery resumed.[351]

The deadly fire by the 45th Virginia shoved the blue-clad troopers back a short distance. "I tell you I done some running and hollowing after them until I came to a house in a bottom that the enemy had sheltered in," recalled a private of the 45th Virginia.

> *The ground around the house lie so thick with dead and clothes burnt off of them there was barley room to place our feet, it was so sad I quit yelling. Next we passed a house on side of road with amputated limbs thrown out at the window as large as hay stacks. Next we came to dismounted cannons in a little bottom and artillery horses with their rumps shot off which showed the destructive work of our cannons.*[352]

Patton also reported that the blue-clad horse soldiers maintained a brisk small-arms fire until late morning, when his troops repulsed another "ineffectual" attack.[353] Major R.A. Bailey, now in command of the 22nd Virginia Infantry, left an especially colorful description of the action on the morning of August 27: "At daybreak of the 27th, the enemy opened on us again and kept up a spirited fire until about 11 a.m., when they again attempted to form and charge us; but were whipped, scattered, and driven in disorder back before they could form."[354]

After Patton repulsed that final attack, Lieutenant Colonel John J. Polsley of the 8th West Virginia reported that the enemy was moving to flank Averell's rear.[355] With this unwelcome news, Averell realized that his men were desperately low on ammunition and that Scammon's troops were not going to make it to the battlefield in time to tip the balance.[356] Left with no alternative, Averell ordered the withdrawal of his command at about 10:30 a.m.[357] The blue-clad horse soldiers bore off all of their wounded who could be transported and left the rest behind in the care of assistant surgeon C.M. Worthington of the 14th Pennsylvania Cavalry.[358]

It would be a fighting withdrawal. Averell had his cannons double-shotted with the last rounds of canister, ready to tear gaping holes in the ranks of any Confederates who might try to pursue.[359] By 11:15 a.m., his column was

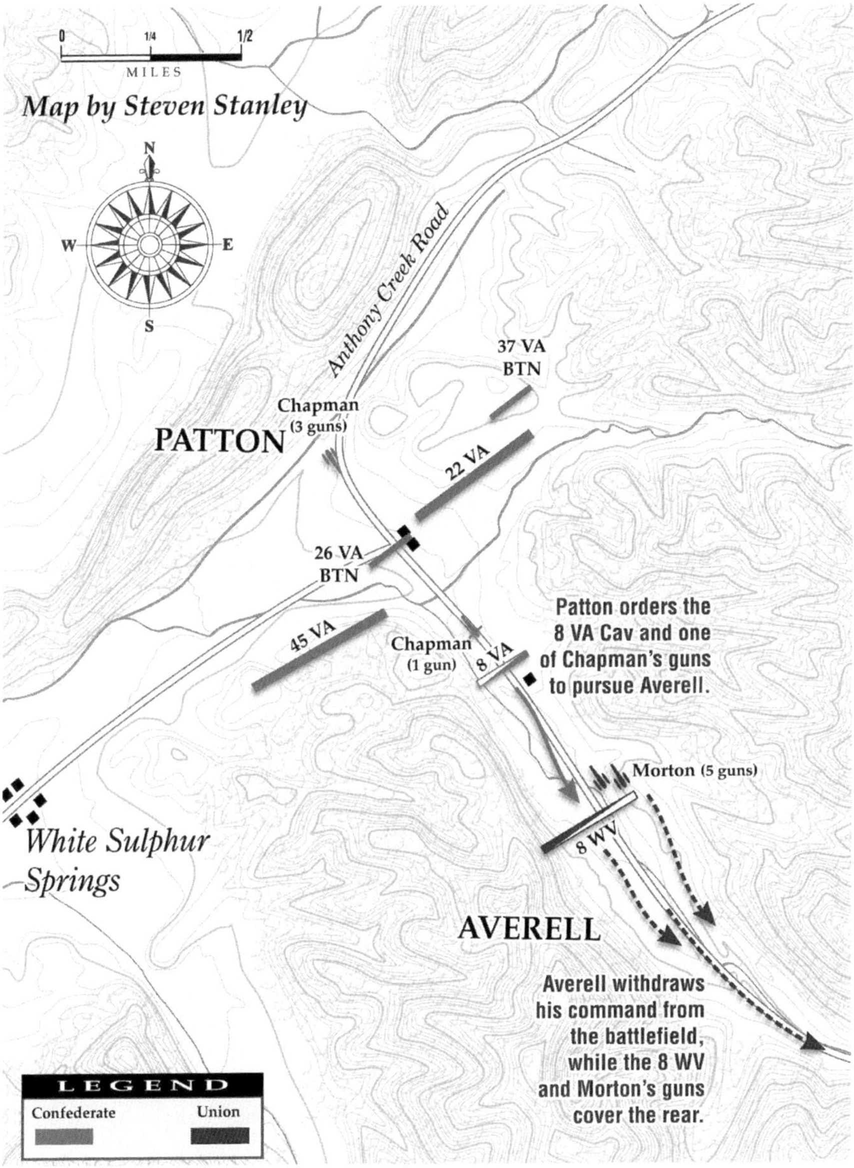

Averell withdraws.

moving off in good order, with his rear guard manning the barricades in an effort to buy time for the main body to reach safety.[360] "When the enemy came up our rear guard stationed behind the fallen trees gave them a warm reception," declared an officer of the 2nd West Virginia.[361] The double-shotted cannons belched fire and then limbered up and rode off, leaving torn, bleeding Confederate bodies in their wake.[362]

Averell ordered the 8th West Virginia to cover the retreat, to move slowly over the hill and to their horses, which were being held on the back of the slope. "This we did, and found the other regiments falling back slowly and in good order," recounted a captain of the 8th West Virginia. "We came to the narrows, and formed in line of battle across the ravine, with skirmishers on the hill, and in a short time our pioneers had a barricade of timber across the road over which cavalry or artillery could not pass until removed." The men had to search for their horses, which were scattered along the road for nearly six miles. When they found their steeds, they mounted. "By the time we reached the gap we were all mounted and moving in good order, and except the noble men that we left with sorrow, we felt that we were in condition to meet the enemy again."[363]

Patton ordered George Edgar to advance his skirmishers, and the men of the 26th Battalion advanced cautiously until it became obvious that Averell's men had abandoned their positions in Edgar's front.[364] The Union rear guard repulsed two more attacks by Patton's men before withdrawing from the battlefield. The Federal troopers constructed successive barricades as they withdrew, permitting Averell to fall all the way back to Callaghan with little hindrance before halting to rest his weary men and horses.[365]

Patton ordered his cavalry and artillery to pursue the retreating Federals. "For about 10 or 12 miles the road passes through a very narrow and thickly wooded defile," reported Major General Sam Jones. "The enemy availed himself of the advantage offered to retard pursuit by felling trees across the road. I was informed that he had left a regiment of infantry and a squadron of cavalry at the Warm Springs, and under the assumption that he would make a stand at the latter place, the First Brigade was pushed forward in pursuit. The enemy, however, turned off from the direct road at Morris's Hill and retreated rapidly by way of Huntersville toward Beverly."[366]

However, Lieutenant Mathew Wilson and his Company L of the 14th Pennsylvania Cavalry had been sent to hold a position near the Miller house, and nobody had bothered to tell Wilson that the main body of the Fourth Separate Brigade was leaving. Wilson, age thirty-three, was known as "a gallant man, a courageous officer, and model Christian patriot." This day he found himself in a difficult position. Sergeant Joshua Groft, one of Wilson's men, discovered that the rest of the Union army had left and reported this unwelcome news to Lieutenant Wilson. Wilson feared that if they left, they would all be killed, and he was inclined to wait it out. Groft disagreed and told Wilson that he would take command and get the men out. All but Wilson and two other men escaped. Wilson was wounded and captured, and his two comrades were captured.[367]

Groft and his detachment headed for the woods, dodging Confederate Minié balls as they ran—"and how they did make the balls dance around us," he recalled. "When at last we came to the fence I did not take time to climb over it, but just threw myself on the top rail and fell over it, and when I struck the ground I believe a half dozen balls must have struck the top rail." Groft found himself alone in the woods and, coming upon a full kettle of coffee, paused for a moment to help himself to the welcome refreshments. He finally came across the Union barricade and rejoined the retreating column, making it back safely. "The rebels did not follow us very far," he noted, "and I think that they were as badly used up as ourselves."[368]

Hamilton Smith, also of Wilson's company, was not so lucky as Groft. Smith watched the withdrawal of the bulk of the command and asked a couple of the older men in his company if the Federals had left the field and was told that they had. "I am going too," declared Smith. They replied, "You will never get out." Smith replied, "I am going, goodbye." He took off running as fast as he could. Before long, Confederate bullets began whizzing by, buzzing like angry bees. Smith dropped to his hands and knees and rolled into a fence corner, where he was shot through the right foot. He jumped up and limped off until he reached a deep ravine and spotted William Stevenson of his company climbing the opposite bank. Smith called for Stevenson to wait for him and to take his arms. Stevenson helped Smith up the bank, and they ran across the field to the position previously held by Morton's artillery.

Two others of his company, Lieutenant S.D. Hazlett and Joseph Mateer, joined them there. Both Hazlett and Mateer were wounded and were making their way to the field hospital for treatment. By now, Smith was growing weak and thirsty from loss of blood, and he paused to take a drink as they crossed a small stream. He reached the field hospital and had his wound dressed, but he, along with the other men being treated there, was captured and left to the tender mercies of the victorious Confederates.[369]

Colonel Patton described the efforts to pursue by his troops. He detailed Colonel James M. Corns and his five companies of the 8th Virginia Cavalry, one of Chapman's guns and some of his infantry to pursue Averell's retreating column. Patton ordered Corns to mount his five companies as rapidly as possible and to pursue the enemy. "It was soon found, however, that the enemy had so heavily blockaded in their rear that much delay would be experienced," Patton reported, his frustration obvious. "Pioneer parties were detailed to cut out the blockade, and very early the next morning the cavalry started again in pursuit, the infantry also moving as far as Callaghan, when it was found that the enemy had passed Gatewood's, where it had been hoped they would have been intercepted by Colonel Jackson's command."[370]

The strength of the Union barricades also frustrated Corns. "Such were their facilities for filling the road with timber, and the formation of the country being such that it was impossible to get around the blockade with cavalry, I was compelled to give up the pursuit until morning," he wrote. "Having left a company of my command to cut out the blockade during the night, and also to watch the movements of the enemy, I returned to Dry Creek, the nearest point at which I could get forage for my horses and provisions for my men."[371] Corns's being forced to give up the pursuit by the stout barricades cast the die: from that moment forward, the Confederates would be well behind Averell's column, desperately trying to catch up.

Sergeant John Stevens of Chapman's battery joined the halfhearted pursuit. After inspecting the damaged gun abandoned by Morton's battery, Stevens came upon a house that had been used as a field hospital for wounded Union soldiers. "The lower side of this cottage rested on posts about six or seven feet high to bring the floor level with the pike, and under the windows of same were great piles of amputated arms and legs, thrown out by the surgeons of the enemy in their rapid work," reported a horrified Stevens. "I, personally, saw several legs with the trousers and shoes or boots still on them, the surgeons evidently having no time to remove clothing before operating." Stevens noted that "after pursuing the enemy a few miles and seeing the futility of endeavoring further pursuit over a road which their pioneers had so thoroughly blockaded, were countermarched to the field of battle for a short rest, and to count up casualties—which were not a few, for our small force—and considerably more on the part of the enemy."[372]

Jones desperately tried to cut off Averell's route of march. He informed Imboden that Averell and Patton had tangled again that day and that Averell had withdrawn in the direction of Warm Springs. "They suffered severely here, and are much exhausted, both men and horses, and I believe they are short of ammunition," reported Jones. "Look for them and damage them as much as possible." He told Mudwall Jackson to "push them to the utmost, and help destroy them if possible." Finally, Jones also ordered the brigades of Ferguson and Wharton to move as quickly as possible toward Warm Springs, where they were to attack Averell.[373]

That night, Sam Jones issued a congratulatory order to his victorious troops:

> *The major-general commanding tenders his cordial congratulations and thanks to the troops for their gallantry and good conduct yesterday and to-day. After a fatiguing march of twenty-four consecutive hours, they encountered the enemy in largely superior numbers, and from 9 o'clock in the morning repelled repeated and bold charges of infantry and cavalry, supported by a heavy fire of artillery, with a steadiness and spirit worthy of the highest praise. Again this morning they repelled handsomely two attacks, and forced the enemy to abandon his position and retreat in haste.*
>
> *In this engagement the Forty-fifth and Twenty-second Regiments and Twenty-third and Twenty-sixth Battalions Virginia Infantry, the Eighth Regiment and Thirty-seventh Battalion Virginia Cavalry, and Chapman's battery, inscribed their names high on the roll of those who in this war have illustrated the valor of our troops.*
>
> *No one can regard it as an invidious distinction to mention particularly the commander of the First Brigade, Col. G.S. Patton. He exhibited admirable judgment in placing his troops in action, and his gallantry was conspicuous throughout the day.*
>
> *The enemy, though in retreat, is not beyond our lines. He must be driven beyond them. With devout thanks to Almighty God for the victory He has given us, and humble trust in Him, let us press on and complete the work so happily done.*[374]

Jones's exhortations notwithstanding, Patton's weary infantrymen failed to catch up to Averell's troopers and likewise failed to drive them from beyond the Confederate lines. However, Averell had no plans to stay within their lines—out of ammunition and stymied, he had to fall back to his base of supplies and operations.

The Virginia newspapers celebrated the Confederate victory. "The repulse of the enemy was decisive, and our forces were in hot pursuit, picking up prisoners rapidly," reported the *Richmond Daily Dispatch*. "No further apprehensions are felt that the enemy will be able to reach the Tennessee Railroad with their present force," continued the article. "They have been effectually checked, and have suffered to such an extent as to make another attempt by the same party entirely out of the question."[375]

After the Federals abandoned the battlefield, Patton and his men were left to care for several hundred dead and wounded men of both sides. That afternoon, nuns of the Sisters of Charity arrived on the battlefield from their convent in Montgomery County to take over caring for the wounded about the same time that the main body of Patton's brigade marched off the field to return to its base at Lewisburg. The sisters remained there for three days, nursing the wounded. Most of the wounded were treated at the Greenbrier, and many of them still remained there as late as November 7, when the last few were evacuated to the town of White Sulphur Springs in Montgomery County, where the sisters could continue to care for them.[376]

The sisters had their hands full. The battlefield was a terrible place, with dead and wounded men and horses of both sides littered promiscuously about. That night, troopers of the 14th Virginia Cavalry of Colonel Milton J. Ferguson's brigade arrived on the battlefield at White Sulphur Springs, hoping to join the pursuit of Averell's command. "I saw more men killed there than at any other time during the war," recalled Lieutenant James S. McClung of the 14th Virginia. "We had to move men around to ride through there." Ferguson's men arrived too late to provide effective support of the pursuit and eventually made their way to Jones's headquarters at Lewisburg.[377]

Graves of unidentified Confederate casualties of the Battle of White Sulphur Springs on the grounds of the Greenbrier. *Author photo.*

Some of the dead were buried on the battlefield where they

fell. Others were buried in a small family graveyard on the grounds of the Greenbrier Resort, and still others were buried on a hill overlooking the postwar Virginia Central Railroad tracks that now pass through the Greenbrier River Valley. Most of the graves are unmarked, as their occupants are largely unknown, although standard issue Confederate grave markers delineate the remains of the unknown Virginians who rest in those graveyards.[378]

Captain Chatham T. Ewing, the badly wounded Union battery commander, was one of the men too severely injured to be transported with Averell's column, and he was reluctantly left behind to the tender mercies of the Confederates. Sergeant John Stevens of Chapman's battery befriended his fellow artillerist, and the two men spent many hours in interesting conversation. Patton realized that his quartermaster, Major George McKendree, was missing, and he resolved to arrange an exchange cartel of Ewing for McKendree, whom he incorrectly assumed was a prisoner of war.[379]

Lieutenant Noyes Rand, Patton's adjutant, wrote a note that was sent forward under a flag of truce, proposing the exchange. The flag of truce caught up to Averell, and the note was brought to the New Yorker. Averell responded, "I would be more than pleased to accept your proposition, but either fortunately or unfortunately, your Major McKendree is 'absent without leave' but if you will hold Ewing at your headquarters we can possibly agree upon a satisfactory exchange in some other way." McKendree, it turned out, had been hiding and eventually made his way back to safety and rejoined Patton's headquarters. The badly injured Ewing was paroled and left behind to recover from his abdominal wound.[380]

As they so often did, the Confederates used the opportunity to banter with the Union prisoners. "If we had not run out of ammunition we would have whipped you 'Johnnie Rebs,'" declared one Federal soldier. "We know nothing about you running out of ammunition, but we do know you run," retorted a Virginian, to peals of laughter. A different Union soldier responded, "I do not know about us whipping; I tell you that those old Johnnie Reb bullets come singing up the hollow, 'where are you?' 'where are you?' Mighty wicked." The laughter eased the embarrassment for the captured Union soldiers but did little to help them feel better about their plight.[381]

A Virginia newspaper noted that the battlefield was the site of a small settlement whose inhabitants fled to escape the violence of the clash of arms. "Mr. Miller, well known as a merchant at Dry Creek, lost his dwelling house and kitchen, which were set on fire by a shell. In his house was

The Miller house, which was located at the center of the battlefield at White Sulphur Springs. *Steve Cunningham.*

consumed all his money, which was in notes, two gold watches, and his furniture, clothing, &c., his family saving nothing, having left precipitately to escape the dangers of the fight—their house being between the two armies," reported the newspaper. The correspondent also noted that other residents of the settlement at Dry Creek suffered similar losses as a result of the two days when the hard hand of war visited their doorsteps.[382]

Another correspondent claimed that Averell's troopers "treated our citizens in the neighborhood of the battlefield in the most wanton and devilish manner. They destroyed utterly every article of household furniture, broke up into small pieces chairs, cups, plates, dishes, bedsteads, bureaus, &c., tore open the beds and scattered the feathers in the yard, tore up all the bed clothes, &c., wearing apparel, broke the glass out of the windows, and destroyed the clocks even. In a word, not an article of any description was left." The newspaper correspondent also claimed that the Yankees shot the milk cows and took all of the corn, wheat, hay, oats and other grains, leaving the residents of Dry Creek largely destitute. Such was the hard hand of war.[383]

Having successfully driven off the invaders, Sam Jones desperately wanted to catch Averell's command and punish it. The question was whether his forces would be able to do so.

7

Averell's Retreat and the Confederate Pursuit

After conducting a tenacious fighting withdrawal, Averell's weary, hungry men safely arrived at Callaghan's Tavern late on the afternoon of August 27. They built fires and ate their first real meal for the first time in thirty-six long, miserable hours. After resting and enjoying whatever rations they had, the Fourth Separate Brigade resumed the march after sundown, this time heading for Warm Springs. Averell ordered his men to leave their fires burning to create the illusion that they were still there in place to deter the Confederates from continuing to pursue. With a contraband serving as a guide, they took a direct route to the Jackson River Valley, avoiding the winding road to Warm Springs that the Confederates expected them to use.[384]

Once Patton's infantry abandoned the pursuit of the fleeing Union horse soldiers, the primary responsibility for the pursuit fell upon the shoulders of Colonel William L. "Mudwall" Jackson and the 19th and 20th Virginia Cavalry of his command. That morning, Jackson ordered his small detachment of infantry to march to Warm Springs to arrange a warm reception for Averell. Jackson then rode forward himself to take command there. Upon arriving, he heard reports of the fighting at White Sulphur Springs, as well as reports that Patton was falling back in the face of the enemy. He reacted by sending a couple of detachments to move to try to cut off Averell's route of march. Later that morning, Jackson learned that Averell's command had hit the road once more, headed toward Warm Springs, and that he should be on the lookout for it.[385]

On the twenty-eighth, a civilian informed Sam Jones that local citizens were blockading the Jackson River road. Jones saw an opportunity and asked them to complete their barricade in the hope that they would slow down the Union cavalry enough for the 20th Virginia Cavalry to arrive to resist their passage. Jackson ordered the 20th Virginia Cavalry to barricade both the road to Hot Springs and also the Jackson River road. The Southern horse soldiers were in the middle of building their barricades when Jackson learned that Averell had taken a different route and was instead headed toward the Gatewood Plantation in Pocahontas County.[386]

Mudwall Jackson failed miserably in his attempts to follow up the Confederate victory at White Sulphur Springs. His pursuit was halfhearted and not well managed. One of Patton's infantrymen was especially blunt in his criticism of Jackson's performance. "If Jackson had of blocked the road and held them in check until we got to him we would have captured the whole of them," he declared.[387] Whether the Confederates could have bagged Averell's entire command is an open question, but they certainly could have inflicted some serious damage on the blue-clad horse soldiers had Jackson managed to interdict their retreat.

Colonel James M. Corns of the 8th Virginia Cavalry, a thirty-four-year-old Welshman and former prisoner of war who had only recently been exchanged in order to return to duty, described the poor effort made by Jackson:[388]

> *At 5 a.m. on the 28th, at the hour indicated, I started with five companies of my command and a portion of the Thirty-seventh Battalion, in command of Major* [James R.] *Claiborne, and finding, through my scouts, that the enemy had left Callaghan's about 2 o'clock in the night, I pushed on rapidly with the hope that Colonel Jackson, who I understood was at the Warm Springs, would so blockade the roads and otherwise delay the enemy's retreat as to enable me to come up with him; and it is the opinion of all of my officers and myself that had 100 men been thrown down the road leading from the Warm Springs turnpike to Gatewood's, that they could have so obstructed the road in two hours' time as to have compelled the enemy to abandon all of his transportation and cannon, and perhaps to surrender his entire command.*[389]

Some of Mudwall Jackson's troopers attempted to spread disinformation that might trick Averell and mentioned to some of the local citizens that the main body of Jackson's cavalry was at Gatewood in force. However, this was a ruse, and Averell saw through it quickly and easily. "This shallow attempt at deception did not deter us from marching to that point, where we arrived at daylight on the 29th," he declared.[390]

In the meantime, Colonel Corns pushed his weary troopers as hard and as far as he could. When they were within six miles of the Gatewood Plantation, Corns received a dispatch from Jackson stating that the enemy

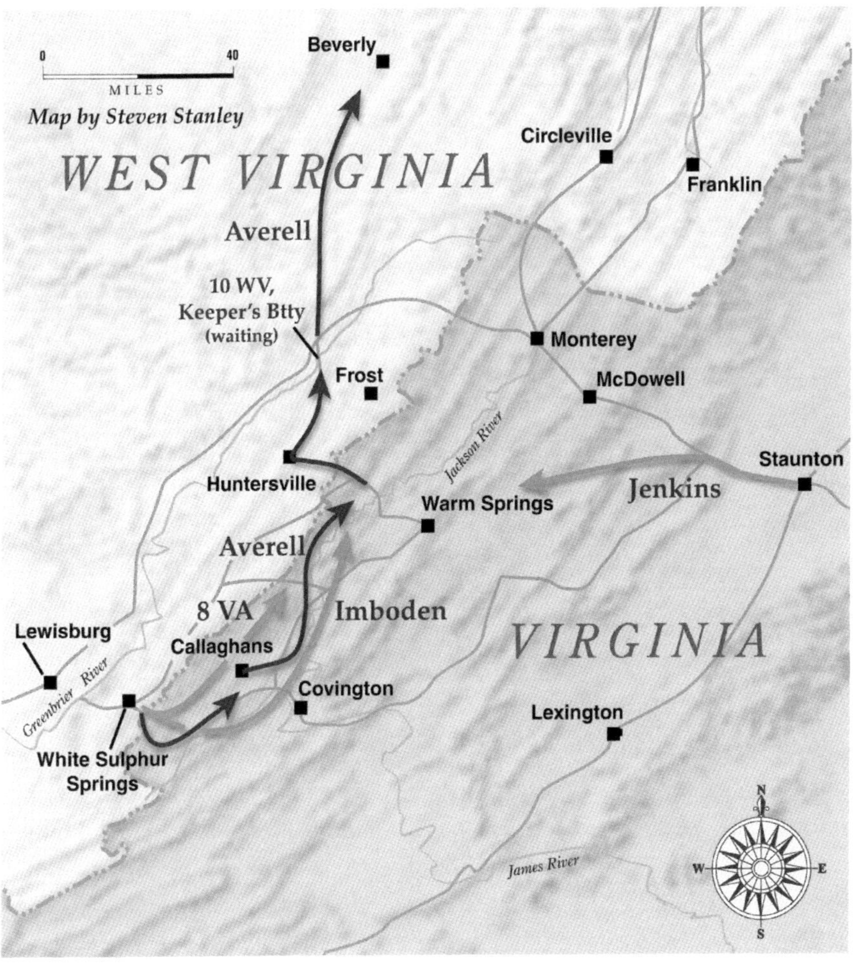

Averell's return route and the Confederate pursuit.

had passed out of the road where Corns had hoped to intercept Averell's column and had passed Gatewood on the way to Huntersville. Corns made it as far as Gatewood but found it impossible to go farther—his horses were at the limits of their endurance and needed to be fed and rested. With no alternative, Corns halted to feed his horses. Not long after unsaddling to feed, Corns received an order from Sam Jones to join with Mudwall Jackson in a vigorous pursuit of the enemy. Corns obeyed the order immediately and marched for Huntersville. However, they arrived too late to catch the New Yorker and his weary horse soldiers.[391]

Averell permitted his tired command a few hours of much-needed rest and then moved out again at 9:00 a.m. Colonel W.W. Arnett and his 20th Virginia Cavalry, which had pushed its pursuit of Averell's column, came up just short. "Colonel Arnett arrived at Gatewood's in time to fire on the pickets and see the rear of the enemy in rapid retreat," reported a frustrated Mudwall Jackson, "and following them to Little Black Creek, he turned to the right across the mountain to blockade the Knapp's Creek road." However, Averell had slipped away again.[392]

The Federal horse soldiers marched all the way to Huntersville without interruption, having covered sixty miles in about twenty-eight hours.[393] However, much like their march south, angry bushwhackers constantly plagued the march north. Bushwhackers wounded a trooper of the 14th Pennsylvania Cavalry that morning and killed another two.[394] "It was a fearful march, without rest, and constantly harassed by the bushwhackers, who seemed to be in every wooded place, whence they sent into our columns the death dealing bullets," described a member of the 2nd West Virginia. "There was not the slightest opportunity to defend ourselves, and it was warfare that was devoid of the excitement of the battle field, hence the harder to bear."[395]

Jackson's weary troopers pushed on, and his advance elements ran into Averell's pickets at Huntersville, discovering "the enemy there apparently intending to make a stand in supporting distance of the infantry regiment that had been left in their rear," reported Jackson. After allowing the weary horsemen of the 20th Virginia Cavalry a few hours to rest and feed their horses, Jackson ordered Colonel Arnett and his men to make a nighttime advance and get into position to attack Averell. However, when the Confederate cavalry arrived at their destination, they discovered that the Federals were, once more, gone. By now, Jackson's frustration was palpable.[396]

Colonel Milton J. Ferguson, commanding Jenkins's brigade of cavalry. *Terry Lowry.*

Brigadier General John D. Imboden, commander of the Northwestern Cavalry Brigade. *USAHEC.*

As dusk fell, Averell's command moved out again, headed for the only bridge over the Greenbrier River, the Greenbrier Bridge (located at modern Marlinton—6.5 miles from Huntersville), where Colonel Thomas M. Harris and his 10th West Virginia Infantry awaited their arrival with a herd of cattle and plenty of good fodder for the horses.[397] "The powers of endurance of both men and horses were tried to the utmost," recalled a captain of the 8th West Virginia, "and during that night's march a number of our worn-down horses were abandoned and the exhausted men would sleep in their saddles."[398]

With the infantry to protect them, the exhausted men and horses of the Fourth Separate Brigade bivouacked for the night.[399] The 10th West Virginia had captured a substantial herd of cattle, and they also had Averell's wagon trains with them, so the troopers enjoyed a good meal of fresh meat for the first time in days. "Here we enjoyed a good night's rest, and had such dreams as only tired soldiers can have."[400] Benjamin Ronk of Company I of the 8th West Virginia arrived in Huntersville with his regiment. However, "on arriving here I was so worn out with the rheumatism I here got past riding and was put in a wagon and hauled to Beverly," the exhausted man scrawled in his diary.[401]

Averell did not know it, but large contingents of Confederate troops were pursuing him. Colonel Milton J. Ferguson's cavalry brigade was on its way to Warm Springs from Staunton, and Brigadier General John D. Imboden's mounted brigade was trying to race Averell to Huntersville. However, Averell's lead was insurmountable, and Major General Sam Jones correctly predicted that Imboden would not get to Huntersville in time to intercept Averell. However, with some satisfaction, Jones noted that Averell's command "have been severely punished, and when they reach Beverly will not, I think, be fit for service for several weeks."[402]

Mudwall Jackson's command nearly caught up to Averell at Huntersville. His advance guard probed at the Union defenses and "discovered the enemy there apparently intending to make a stand in supporting distance of the infantry regiment which had been left in their rear," reported Jackson. Since it was dark, Jackson decided to bivouac near the ruins of Camp Northwest, and that decision allowed the Fourth Separate Brigade to slip from his fingers. When his troopers advanced on Huntersville the next morning, they overcame yet another barricade constructed by Averell's troopers only to learn that the blue-clad horse soldiers had already moved on.[403]

Colonel James M. Corns and his five companies of the 8th Virginia Cavalry caught up to Jackson and his three hundred infantry, who were "very much broken down by the long march from Camp Northwest to Millborough and back to Huntersville." Corns pressed on to Marlinboro but discovered that Averell's rear guard had left two hours earlier. With that, Corns gave up. "My command being in no condition to pursue, most of the horses being broken down and barefooted, I concluded to come back to camp through Pocahontas [County] by the way of Frankford."[404]

Jackson made one last attempt to cut off Averell on August 30, but his command's mounts were too worn out to accomplish much. Only a small detachment of Arnett's 20th Virginia Cavalry managed to catch up to Averell's column. Arnett blockaded the road and posted some of his men, who delayed and fired upon the Federals, but his force was too small to accomplish much more than that. Thus, the halfhearted Confederate pursuit ended in frustration. Jackson concluded his report of the raid by claiming, "Regretting that I did not accomplish more, but respectfully submitting that, with all the means and information before me, I accomplished all that was possible."[405] He ordered Jenkins's Brigade to march to and occupy McDowell, where the brigade's horses would find plenty of good grass for grazing.[406]

In addition, a new threat loomed. Jones learned that Major General Ambrose E. Burnside and his Ninth and Twenty-third Corps were advancing on Knoxville, Tennessee. Burnside's large army of twenty-one thousand men posed a far greater threat than did Averell's small, battered, retreating brigade. Jones had to deal with this new danger—and quickly.[407] With that new, major hazard to contend with, Sam Jones called off the pursuit of Averell's command.

The Union horse soldiers were hungry and exhausted.[408] After so many days on the march with little in the way of rations or forage, both men and horses were in bad shape and nearing the limits of their endurance. "We knew that Jones, with all the forces that he could raise, would follow in pursuit, and there was a probability that Imboden would try to cut off our retreat at the mouth of the Elkwater, but we were resolved to cut our way through," recalled a West Virginian, contemplating the ordeal of the next day's march. The men grimly prepared to move out.[409]

The Union column moved out at 2:00 a.m. on August 30. At daylight, they encountered a barricade, half a mile long and constructed of felled trees across a road, in an effort to delay the Fourth Separate Brigade's advance long enough for Mudwall Jackson's cavalry to fall upon them.[410] Averell detailed some of his command to attack the barricade with axes, while the rest of his brigade used the opportunity to feed their horses and to build their own strong blockade across their rear in case the Confederates persisted in trying to pursue them. It took about an hour to clear the barricade. They still had another sixty miles to go to reach safety at Beverly. After a long day's march, Averell and his command camped for the night about ten miles from their destination of Beverly.[411]

The Fourth Separate Brigade finally arrived at Beverly—the starting point of the raid—about 11:00 a.m. on August 31. After twenty-seven days in the saddle, the long raid was finally over.[412] "I arrived at Beverly on August 31 with the rest of the brigade after a fatiguing march of 125 miles," reported Colonel John Oley of the 8th West Virginia.[413]

"Averell and his command, when last heard from, were 15 miles beyond Huntersville, going rapidly toward Beverly, followed by a few of Jackson's men, all infantry," reported Sam Jones. "Cavalry support, which he met at Huntersville, will probably shield him from further punishment, unless Imboden intercepts him at Huntersville. I think the blow aimed at us from that direction, with Averell to direct it, has been very effectually parried," he proudly declared.[414]

At the same time, Patton's critical defeat of Averell at White Sulphur Springs left the Fourth Separate Brigade "so crippled, it was believed, as to relieve any apprehension of danger from him for a month or two," correctly noted Jones. The repulse of Averell's raid permitted Jones to turn to meet the threat posed by Burnside's army. Jones sent "a part of his troops to the defense of southwestern Virginia. [Brigadier General Gabriel C.] Wharton's brigade...was ordered to the vicinity of the salt works near Abingdon, and General Jones went to the latter place on September 6."[415] The defeat of Averell at White Sulphur Springs permitted Jones to shift his thinly stretched forces to meet threats.

In spite of being effectually parried, Averell still had every reason to be proud of his troopers, even though their mission to seize the law library had failed. They had spent twenty-seven days on the march, under fire of the enemy or in line of battle for fifteen of those days. They spent twelve of those twenty-seven days without food for men or horses and literally cut or fought their way through 150 miles of Virginia and West Virginia wilderness. The long, arduous raid had been quite an ordeal for both men and horses.[416]

"The command arrived at Beverly on August 31, having marched, since June 10, some 636 miles, exclusive of the distance passed over by railroad and of the marches made by detachments, which would increase the distance for the entire command to at least 1,000 miles," proudly wrote William Woods Averell. "This command has been mounted, equipped, and drilled; has marched over 600 miles through a rugged mountainous region, fighting the enemy almost daily; had one severe battle; destroyed the camps of the enemy; captured large amounts of supplies and 266 prisoners, in less than eighty days."[417]

8

An Assessment of the Battle of White Sulphur Springs

With the long raid finally over, Brigadier General William Woods Averell wrote a congratulatory order to his Fourth Separate Brigade. Each regiment got the same order, only altered for the specific regiment involved. This is the order to the 14th Pennsylvania Cavalry:

> *The General commanding the Fourth Separate Brigade desires to express to the officers and men of the 14th Pennsylvania Cavalry, who took part into the recent expedition into the country occupied by the enemy his high appreciation of the fortitude and gallantry you have displayed. You sought the enemy in his own stronghold, and drove him from confusion from his camp, destroying his military resources throughout a vast region. Relying upon co-operation of other forces which had been promised to you, but which did not come, you attacked superior forces of the enemy with an impetuosity which dislodged him from his first position, and success was dawning upon your arms when lack of ammunition obliged you to pause. Even then you stood fast witnessing the fall of many noble comrades with a fortitude that the reinforcements of the enemy could not disturb.*
>
> *When directed to withdraw you retired with the dignity of soldiers baffled, but not beaten. You have encountered cold and hunger, and the numerous shots of lurking cowards have been met with the indifference of tried courage. The combined efforts of the enemy failed to make you propose, or to prevent your return.*

Let the grief which fills our hearts for our fallen comrades and friends render them stout in a just cause. Prepare at once for greater undertakings.[418]

Averell had every reason to be proud of these men, who had only been converted to cavalry a few months earlier and who had no prior experience with such a trying expedition.

"I could but admire the conduct of our men," proudly echoed a captain of the 8th West Virginia. "During the whole march I did not hear a single man grumble, and they were perfectly indifferent to the cowardly attacks of the bushwhackers, except some indignant expression of what they would like to do if they only had them in their power."[419] A member of the 3rd West Virginia sounded a similar note. "We were not whipped, but held our ground until a lack of shooting material compelled us to retreat. If we had been supplied with ammunition, the victory would surely have been ours," he declared. "The fault lies at some man's door, not with the brave soldiers who were in the fight."[420]

Not surprisingly, the Confederate newspapers took a much different view of events. "The Yankees under the great raider Averill took a summer jaunt to the White Sulphur Springs for the benefit of their health and met with such a warm and cordial reception that many of them concluded to remain and take up their bounty land, but finally concluded to be satisfied with six feet by two of ground, instead of a quarter section," colorfully proclaimed one Virginia broadsheet.[421]

Lieutenant Colonel George M. Edgar, commander of the 23rd Battalion of Virginia Infantry, whose command bore the brunt of the fighting at White Sulphur Springs, weighed in. "Of all the battles of the Civil War, fought in the Department of Western Virginia, none were more prolonged, more stubbornly fought, more creditable of the commanding officer and his subordinate officers of all arms, or to the rank and file, or more interesting in their details than that of White Sulphur Springs, Dry Creek, or Rocky Gap, as it has been variously called."

Edgar continued, "It was unique, too, both in the purpose of the expedition in which it was the chief incident, and in the successful use of infantry in intercepting and defeating a large body of cavalry and mounted infantry, aided only by a battery of four guns and a few hundred cavalry, hurried to the field in the progress of the fight—the whole aggregating barely two-thirds of the strength of the opposing force."[422] Edgar apparently never realized that Patton's force significantly outnumbered Averell's. However, the rest of his points remain valid, particularly in discussing the importance of slower infantry being used to bring cavalry to bay.

Both sides suffered heavy losses. Indeed, many men of both sides paid with their lives. Averell reported 3 officers and 28 enlisted men killed, 11 officers and 114 enlisted men wounded and 1 officer and 66 enlisted men captured or missing, for total losses of 218, which represented 17 percent of his total command.[423] Patton reported 2 officers and 18 enlisted men killed, 11 officers and 118 enlisted men wounded and 18 enlisted men missing or captured, for total losses of 162, representing losses of about 7 percent of his total command.[424] Given the relatively small numbers of command, the heavy losses reflect the ferocity of the combat that raged at White Sulphur Springs for a day and a half that hot August.

Colonel James M. Schoonmaker eloquently summed up the nature of the battle at White Sulphur Springs in a letter to J.H. Slocum, then the manager of the Greenbrier Resort, in November 1914. "It will be noted that with the exception of my regiment, all of the soldiers in both armies were Virginians," he said, "and in subsequent conference with men engaged on both sides, all agreed that it was one of the hardest fought battles of the Civil War." Schoonmaker concluded by suggesting to Slocum, "The proximity of the battlefield should make it an additional attraction to your beautiful and historic resort."[425] Sadly, and as described below, Schoonmaker's prediction about the battlefield providing an additional attraction for the Greenbrier proved wrong.

An early historian of Chapman's Battery left an apt and accurate description of the battle: "The battle of Dry Creek was one of the hottest, for the numbers engaged, of the war. It was claimed at the time by the Federals to be a drawn battle, but its effect was to turn back Averell's army and preserve for many months a large scope of valuable territory from the devastations of Yankee invasion."[426]

Chapman's gunners, in particular, deserved accolades. The Confederate artillery—often inconsistent in performance—fought long and hard at White Sulphur Springs. Major William McLaughlin, Sam Jones's chief of artillery, praised them in his report of the battle. "The men of the battery stood bravely and steadily by their guns, though subjected to a steady, hot, and well-directed fire from the enemy's guns," he declared, "and too much credit cannot be awarded to Captain Chapman for the zeal, gallantry, and energy displayed by him throughout the engagement."[427]

To a man, Patton's regimental commanders praised the efforts of their units. Their stout stand had stopped Averell's raid about a dozen miles short of its objective and had saved the law library from capture. In the process, they inflicted heavy losses on the Fourth Separate Brigade. "Notwithstanding the great disadvantages under which they labored, the officers and men acted most nobly, repelling the oft-repeated and daring attempts of the enemy to dislodge them," reported Major R. Augustus Bailey of the 22nd Virginia Infantry in a good example of the sort of encomia heaped out on the Confederate soldiers. "The commanders of companies and their subaltern officers are entitled to much praise for their coolness under fire and the tenacity with which they held their ground."[428] A Virginia newspaper sounded a similar note: "All our troops behaved most gallantly, showing great coolness, courage, and power of endurance."[429]

Fielding R. Cornett of Company C of the 8th Virginia Cavalry summed up the role played by the First Brigade in just a few words. "They made ten different charges on our lines," he proudly wrote to his sweetheart, "and would get [with]in ten steps of our men, but were repulsed every time."[430] Such was the nature of the brutal two-day slugging match at White Sulphur Springs.

Patton likewise had every reason to be proud of the performance of his men. "During the engagement I repulsed eight separate and distinct charges of the enemy, besides frequent engagements with his skirmishers," reported Colonel William H. Browne of the 45th Virginia Infantry, who heaped praise on his hard-pressed regiment. "In a majority of these charges the enemy came within the distance of fifteen or twenty paces of my line, and I am well satisfied I did him great damage, capturing some, killing and wounding large numbers. Notwithstanding the long marches my men had made (having marched about 100 miles during the four days preceding the engagement), I had no stragglers or skulkers. I have never on any battlefield seen men act cooler or braver; they fought with a determination to do or die."[431]

These men were all Virginians, and they had sworn their allegiance to the Confederate government at Richmond. Their home county—Greenbrier County—was about to break off from the Commonwealth of Virginia as part of the new state of West Virginia, and they were determined to do anything that they could to prevent that from happening. They were mostly farmers, merchants and students who had enlisted in counties that eventually made up West Virginia. They had no choice in the formation of the new state, and they did not favor it. They strongly believed in the cause of secession, and they were willing to die for a cause that they fervently believed in. Hence, they had an extra incentive to fight hard at White Sulphur Springs, and fight hard they did.

At White Sulphur Springs, George Patton proved to be an able battlefield tactician capable of performing well in independent command. He used his troops well, timely and effectively shifting them to meet threats as they developed. He used his artillery judiciously and efficiently and made outstanding use of difficult terrain that favored the positions held by the enemy. By so doing, he demonstrated that he was a worthy successor to Brigadier General John Echols, whose ongoing health problems forced him to leave the army shortly after the May 5, 1864 Battle of New Market.[432]

Echols heartily endorsed Patton's promotion to brigadier general. He called Patton "energetic, ardent and most effective…prompt, vigilant & highly intelligent, possessing the confidence and affection of his men…a gentleman of high order of accomplishment."[433] Echols's departure made it possible for Patton to become the permanent commander of the First Brigade. His superiors recommended him for promotion to brigadier general in December 1863 as a result of the combination of Echols's ongoing health problems and Patton's fine performance at White Sulphur Springs. However, the Confederate Senate never confirmed the promotion, and he remained a colonel for what remained of his life.[434]

Patton was low key about his role in winning the battle. "I was in command of our forces during the fight and was fortunate enough to escape unhurt," was all he said about it in a letter to a friend a few weeks later.[435] However, George Patton had just over a year to live—he was mortally wounded in action at the September 19, 1864 Third Battle of Winchester—and he remained in command of the First Brigade until his death. During that time, he and his old friend Averell tangled several more times with mixed results. Of course, George S. Patton's greatest legacy was his grandson and namesake, General George S. Patton Jr., who led the Third Army to victory in the European Theater of Operations during World War II.

More important, Patton's defeat of Averell's thrust toward Lewisburg had considerable strategic consequences. During the entirety of Averell's great law book raid, Major General William S. Rosecrans's Army of the Cumberland was in the midst of its brilliant campaign to take the vital rail hub of Chattanooga, which fell to Rosecrans on September 9, just over a week after Averell's raid ended. The fall of Chattanooga so alarmed the

Confederate high command that Lieutenant General James Longstreet's First Corps, Army of Northern Virginia, was sent to reinforce General Braxton Bragg's Army of Tennessee, stripping Robert E. Lee's Army of Northern Virginia of a significant portion of its hardened core of veteran soldiers.[436]

Burnside's army forayed into east Tennessee both to secure the territory for the Union loyalists who made up the bulk of that region's population and to tie up Jones's troops and prevent them from being used to further reinforce Bragg's army. Indeed, Burnside intended to recruit and arm additional troops in the area, further enlarging his army.[437] Had Averell defeated Patton and pushed on to Lewisburg, Jones would not have been able to shift his focus from Averell's threat from the east to the threat posed by Burnside's army's approach from the west, and his command would have been badly squeezed. Hence, Patton's victory at White Sulphur Springs had significant strategic consequences for the defense of east Tennessee and also for what soon became known as the Chickamauga Campaign.

At the same time, the lackluster Confederate pursuit of the Fourth Separate Brigade left a lot to be desired. Writing a few days after Averell escaped, General Robert E. Lee penned a letter to gently chastise Brigadier General John D. Imboden. "I regret exceedingly that the enemy escaped with so little damage to himself," he began. "It seems to me the command of Averell should have been more severely punished. Unless we are active in inflicting all the loss we can upon the parties sent on these expeditions, and in using every opportunity of cutting them off, they will continue to be sent out, will desolate the country, and bring great distress upon the people." Lee concluded, "I hope you will be more successful in the future."[438] Lee's assessment was spot on, and with his gentle chiding, he correctly pointed out that a great opportunity to corral and destroy the Fourth Separate Brigade had slipped away, largely due to the lackluster pursuit executed by Mudwall Jackson, Jenkins's Brigade and Corns's 8th Virginia. Imboden's Brigade was probably too far away to have had much of an opportunity to cut off or otherwise hinder the escape of Averell's command. Nevertheless, Lee was correct—an opportunity to punish the Yankee horse soldiers slipped away due to bungling by Jones's subordinates.

Indeed, his ineffective and inefficient efforts to stop Averell on the way to White Sulphur Springs and his even more ineffective efforts to pursue Averell earned Jackson the unflattering moniker of Mudwall. While pursuing Averell through Huntersville, his troopers found "Mudwall Jackson" scrawled on the walls of the old county courthouse, "the principal feature of which was a complaint that 'Mudwall Jackson' would not fight," as Confederate soldier John McNeel reported. McNeel saw this graffiti a few days after Averell's men evacuated Huntersville, "and it was understood by the Confederate soldiers as having been put there by a Yankee soldier, and as we Confederates understood it at the time, the animus of the verse was because the dead 'Stonewall' had been so hard on the Yankees, and the live 'Mudwall' had escaped their net."[439] The many deficiencies of Jackson's command, which thwarted its efforts to hinder Averell's advance or to catch up to his retreat, made their commander something of a laughingstock. Jackson carried that unhappy nickname for the rest of the war.[440]

Further, Averell conducted his command and the battle well both on the battlefield and during the retreat. His brigade was outnumbered by a large margin, and his men went into battle with an extremely limited supply of ammunition. He used his troops well, was judicious in his use of his limited supply of ammunition and was definitely the aggressor throughout the fight, somewhat uncharacteristically for the normally conservative New Yorker. However, his desire to either wait out Patton or wait for the arrival of Scammon's infantrymen cost his command. "We remained twelve hours longer at Rocky Gap than was necessary, expecting an operation from the Kanawha valley, but it did not come," Captain Francis Mathers of the 8th West Virginia observed.[441]

At the same time, Averell's withdrawal under fire—always difficult under even the best of circumstances—was conducted brilliantly. His planning for the retreat was impeccable, and the execution of his plan was flawless. The barricading of the road made an aggressive pursuit by the outnumbered Confederate cavalry almost impossible, and the use of those barricades bought him sufficient time to safely conduct his entire command to Beverly without any significant exposure to enemy forces. His retreat was a masterpiece, and he deserves a great deal of credit for extracting his command intact while low on ammunition and deep in hostile territory.

Averell took a raw, undisciplined command and turned it into a powerful and effective fighting force in a short period of time. Just a few months earlier, Major Theodore F. Lang of the 3rd West Virginia had described the Fourth Separate Brigade as consisting of "loyal, courageous fighters, scattered through half a dozen counties, but who knew little of discipline, or of regimental or brigade maneuvers—scantily supplied with approved

Major Theodore F. Lang of the 3rd West Virginia. Lang later documented the role of loyal West Virginians in the Civil War. *Ronnie Tront.*

arms, equipment, clothing, etc." Lang also observed that these men "were inefficient for any reliable defense of the country, and the often hopelessness of any effort to take the offense." He had concluded with the damning statement, "All of the officers and enlisted men alike were war students with no teachers among them of skilled warfare." Within eighty days of taking command of the Fourth Separate Brigade, Averell had crafted "a splendid brigade out of the best quality of raw material" and had mounted the men, trained them and made them into a raiding and fighting force to be reckoned with for the rest of the war.[442]

Not long after Averell's repulse at White Sulphur Springs, the Confederate authorities wisely evacuated the law library from Lewisburg and sent it on to Richmond, thereby removing any further incentives for the Union high command to launch another raid to seize it.[443] Nevertheless, Lewisburg remained in the Union bull's-eye. In November 1863, Averell launched another long raid to destroy or damage the Virginia and Tennessee Railroad in the vicinity of Lynchburg or Dublin. This long raid passed through White Sulphur Springs and Lewisburg and culminated in a battlefield victory for Averell over Echols's brigade—the same brigade that had defeated his troops at White Sulphur Springs—in the November 6 Battle of Droop Mountain.[444] According to Patton family legend, while on the way to Droop Mountain, Averell detailed a sergeant to guard the Patton family and stopped to visit Sue Patton and her children at the family's residence in Lewisburg.[445]

The next month, December 1863, Averell led the Fourth Separate Brigade on what may have been the longest, most arduous and most successful cavalry raid of the war. On December 8, Averell's brigade set out on a raid on the Virginia and Tennessee Railroad's important supply depot at

Salem, Virginia. This spectacular raid destroyed three depots, five bridges, fifteen miles of track and many tons' worth of critical supplies intended for Confederate armies. This long and arduous expedition, much of which was conducted in an ice storm, covered 355 miles over thirteen days with minimal casualties and cemented Averell's reputation as the Union's most successful raider.[446]

The Confederates stopped yet another long raid by Averell's brigade during the May 10, 1864 Battle of Cove Gap during yet another operation directed at cutting the Virginia and Tennessee Railroad that led to the burning of the New River Bridge by the Fourth Separate Brigade. Averell was then appointed to command a division of cavalry in Major General David Hunter's army and remained in command of that division when Major General Philip H. Sheridan's Army of the Shenandoah was formed in August 1864. However, Sheridan unjustly and summarily dismissed Averell from command in September for allegedly failing to obey Sheridan's orders to attack Lieutenant General Jubal A. Early's beaten army in the wake of a victory in the September 22, 1864 Battle of Fisher's Hill. A member of the

This page and next: Modern-day views of the battlefield. *Author photos.*

14th Pennsylvania Cavalry recalled, "The release of General Averell was a great surprise to his command who loved him greatly. He was the very idol of the 14th [Pennsylvania] Cavalry whom he had led into nearly two-score battles, nearly one hundred skirmishes, and more than three-score charges."[447]

James E. Taylor, a Northern newspaper correspondent, watched Averell's departure from Sheridan's camps. The "sight of a big blond general on horseback" caught Taylor's eye, and the correspondent watched Averell in "earnest conversation with a dismounted officer." Taylor had never seen Averell before, and the sight intrigued him. "It was with feelings of melancholy interest I observed him," commented the correspondent, "while speculating on the uncertainties of a military career, for his, up to a fortnight back, was full of promise. Now he clasps his friend's hand and rides away."[448] Sheridan exiled Averell to Wheeling to await further orders that never came. William Woods Averell never commanded troops in the field again.

Nevertheless, the New Yorker, who died a very wealthy man as one of the inventors of hot asphalt, left an indelible imprint on his command and on the Union mounted arm. The units that he trained became very effective and reliable commands that were known for their long and arduous raids. While the great law book raid of August 1863 was a failure, largely due to the determined defense by Patton's brigade of Virginians and a severe shortage of ammunition, Averell demonstrated that his Fourth Separate Brigade was now a force to be reckoned with that would be heard from again.

Today, the battlefield is hardly recognizable as a place where brave men fought and died. It certainly does not serve as an attraction for visitors to the world-famous Greenbrier Resort. The intersection of the Anthony's Creek and James River and Kanawha Turnpike has been dramatically altered by the construction of Interstate 64, which dissects the battlefield. Today, it is the intersection of U.S. Route 60 (the Midland Trail) and West Virginia Route 92. The valley portion of the battlefield, once open farm fields, is now occupied by a strip shopping center anchored by a grocery store.

The veterans erected two monuments on the battlefield—one to the fallen Captain Paul Freiherr von König, who is described in Appendix B, and another to commemorate the battle itself. In the 1990s, the living history unit that portrays the White Sulphur Rifles of Edgar's Battalion erected a small monument to honor the memory of the unit it portrays. The three monuments are grouped together, and a black wrought-iron fence surrounds them. When the monuments to Baron von König and to the battle itself

Monuments on the White Sulphur Springs battlefield. *Author photo.*

were erected, they sat in an open field near the location of the former Miller house and store. Then the shopping center—called the Battlefield Center—was built, and the monuments now sit just outside a busy fast-food restaurant. If one does not know that they are there, they are very easy to miss. The only indication that a battle occurred there is a West Virginia state highway historical marker located at the road intersection.

The main Confederate position remains mostly pristine, as it is a cow pasture that is usually filled with grazing animals. A large metal water tank marks the location of Patton's headquarters. Some of the bluffs occupied by Averell's troops remain largely untouched, but the ridgeline closest to the road intersection has been changed dramatically as a consequence of the recent construction of a bank branch. In short, there is little to indicate that a ferocious two-day battle occurred at that road junction. Virtually nothing suggests the strategic significance of the narrow valley, and there is no interpretation there to assist someone trying to ascertain what occurred there. The lack of any such interpretation is tragic. With nothing to help people understand what happened there, there is really no way to pay proper tribute to the men who gave the last full measure of their devotion to the causes in which they believed on those two hot August days in 1863.

In the end, then, the Battle of White Sulphur Springs has been largely forgotten by history. Perhaps that oversight is the result of the small numbers involved, but the small numbers belie the ferocity of the two-day battle. Patton's victory not only ensured that Greenbrier County remained solidly within the control of the Confederacy, but it also ensured that the important law library situated in Lewisburg was not seized for use by the new state of West Virginia. It demonstrated beyond doubt that George Patton was a capable brigade commander, competent to command troops in independent operations, and it likewise demonstrated William Woods Averell's brilliance as a raider. Most importantly, the Battle of White Sulphur Springs, forgotten as it may be, highlights the schisms that brought about the birth of the state of West Virginia and puts a human face on the conflicts that split Virginians during the Civil War. For those reasons, the Battle of White Sulphur Springs is worthy of commemoration. Hopefully, the publication of this book will be the first step in that direction.

Appendix A

Order of Battle

Battle of White Sulphur Springs, August 26–27, 1863

Union Forces

Middle Military District

Eighth Army Corps

Major General Robert Schenck

Fourth Separate Brigade

Brigadier William Woods Averell

2nd West Virginia Mounted Infantry (Colonel George R. Latham)
3rd West Virginia Mounted Infantry (Lieutenant Colonel Francis Thompson)
8th West Virginia Mounted Infantry (Colonel John H. Oley)
14th Pennsylvania Cavalry (Colonel James M. Schoonmaker)
Independent Cavalry Battalion (Major Thomas Gibson Jr.)
Battery G, 1st West Virginia Light Artillery (Captain Chatham T. Ewing [w]; Lieutenant Howard Morton)

Total: approximately thirteen hundred men

Confederate Forces

Department of East Tennessee

Major General Samuel Jones

First (Echols's) Brigade

Colonel George S. Patton

22nd Virginia Infantry (Lieutenant Colonel Andrew R. Barbee [w]; Major Augustus R. Bailey)
45th Virginia Infantry (Colonel William H. Browne)
23rd Battalion Virginia Infantry (Lieutenant Colonel Clarence Derrick)
26th Battalion Virginia Infantry (Lieutenant Colonel George M. Edgar)
Chapman's Company of Virginia Light Artillery (Captain Beirne Chapman)

Other Forces

8th Virginia Cavalry (Colonel James M. Corns; five companies)
37th Battalion Virginia Cavalry (Major J.R. Claiborne; two hundred men)

Total: approximately twenty-three hundred men

Appendix B

Captain Paul Freiherr von König

On November 19, 1914, the men of the Fourth Separate Brigade dedicated a simple yet elegant monument to the memory of Captain Paul Freiherr von König on the battlefield at White Sulphur Springs. The monument was placed at the spot in the field where von König fell and was buried. Today, that monument sits just outside a Hardee's fast-food restaurant. It was the first thing that I saw on the battlefield, and it drew my interest. I set out to learn what I could of the life of Baron Paul von König and to ascertain why there was a monument to him on the battlefield. The story turned out to be as fascinating as it was difficult to divine. This forgotten hero's story needed to be told, and I realized that this book would not be complete unless I did his story justice.

The family von König dates back to 1477, when the name of a master of a guild first appeared in a document. Then, in 1561, Werner König was born. He became a legal scholar, and Duke Heinrich Julius appointed him as chancellor of the Duchy Braunschweig-Wolfenbüttel. In 1605, Werner acquired estates in Lochtum and Vienenburg, both villages situated in a fertile region at the foot of the Harz Mountains, about thirty miles south of Braunschweig (Brunswick) and about an hour from Hanover. More than four centuries later, the family estate, Edelhof, located in Vienenburg, remains in the hands of Werner's descendants.[449]

When Duke Heinrich Julius died in 1611, Werner König accepted an offer from Count (later Prince) Ernst of Schaumburg to become chancellor of Bückeburg, which at the time was the cultural center of the county Schaumburg. Werner died in 1621. By then, his son Johann was already calling himself *von* König, meaning that someone had ennobled the family. The specific circumstances of the ennobling and the granting of the title Freiherr (which means "baron" in German) are not known.[450]

The von Königs mostly married within the nobility of the surrounding regions and thus became part of the gentry of the Guelph countries of Brunswick and Hanover. As was customary in a patrimonial society, the elder son inherited the familial estate, while the other children were paid a stipend that was insufficient to live on. Consequently, the other sons took positions at the royal court or in the military service, mostly in the Duchy Brunswick–Wolfenbüttel or in the electorate of Hanover (which was in Personal Union with the Kingdom of Great Britain; King George III of England was a Hanoverian). However, this was not an exclusive arrangement and did not exclude service in other German countries. Consequently, the von König family proudly boasts a long history of military service.[451]

Friedrich Wilhelm Freiherr von König was born at the family estate in Vienenburg on March 3, 1800. In 1828, he married Pauline Bornemann, the daughter of an affluent merchant family from Hamburg. They had eight children:

Friedrich Wilhelm Freiherr von König, born on January 30, 1830 (who served as an officer in the Austro-Hungarian army)
Alma, born on April 1, 1832 (whose husband was a Hanoverian colonel)
Valesca, born on February 21, 1835
Edmund Robert August Moritz Freiherr von König, born May 13, 1837
Paul Albert Hermann Freiherr von König, born in 1837
Carl August Robert Freiherr von König, born on June 3, 1841
Maria Emma Adeline Helene, born on May 12, 1843 (whose husband was a Prussian colonel)
Friedrich Wilhelm Ulrich Götz Freiherr von König, born on March 13, 1849[452]

The family lived the life of the aristocracy, but military service became its principal means of employment.

Paul's oldest brother, Friedrich Wilhelm, remembered his younger brother as "a rather wild rider" who had ruined several of their father's horses and misbehaved while in school. The boy was fearless. Baron von König escorted his son to Hamburg and permitted Paul to sign on as a ship's boy on a merchant ship. After the second long voyage to China and Japan, where the ship had barely escaped one typhoon, young Paul found himself face to face with a terrible tempest. Two young ship's boys were stuck on the bowsprit and were unable to return to the deck due to the violence of the typhoon. The captain of the ship offered a reward for the rescue of the boys, but none of the sailors budged. Paul tore off his jacket and shoes, climbed the bowsprit, grabbed the collar of the first boy by the teeth, crawled back on all fours and threw the boy before the captain. He repeated this dangerous journey, rescuing the second boy, and then retreated to his bunk without collecting his reward.[453]

When the ship returned to Hamburg, the captain of the ship reported the boy's exploits to the ship's owner. Impressed by the lad's courage, the owner invited Paul to dine with him at his table the next day. Paul declined, insisting that "he first had to bring ashore the ship's load of rice together with the rest of the crew." Paul returned home soon after for a couple of months, where his brother Friedrich Wilhelm taught him the necessary mathematics to obtain his mate's certificate. Paul then passed the exam and became an officer on a big merchant ship of the America Line.[454] He also apparently served in the British army in Calcutta, India, and then in China and participated in the Siege of Peking during the Second Opium War (1856–1860).[455] After leaving China, von König served as a mercenary in the army of General Justo José de Urquiza, the third president of Argentina, and fought in the 1861 Battle of Buenos Aires, wherein Urquiza's forces defeated a rebel army during a civil war. He then came to the United States to serve in the American Civil War.[456] He was quite a character—the sort of fellow who was addicted to thrill seeking.

Paul's younger brother Carl August Robert, who went by the name Robert, had served in the Second War of Italian Independence and was badly wounded at the 1859 Battle of Solferino. Robert recovered from his wound at the family estate, and when the Civil War broke out, he and Paul set sail to find adventure in America. A fellow Union officer remembered that Paul came to the United States to study military field service.[457] Unlike Paul, who spoke fluent English from his years spent working on American and British ships, Robert's English was rather broken.[458] The brothers landed in New York and set about looking for a regiment to join. "The chief reason for their going in on our side is that they hate Negro slavery," remembered a friend.[459]

Colonel Robert J. Betge, a German immigrant with no prior military service, received authority to recruit a regiment of infantry on July 22, 1861, in the aftermath of the disastrous defeat of the Union army at the First Battle of Bull Run the day before.[460] The unit, designated the 68th Infantry Regiment, New York Volunteers, was also known as the 2nd German Rifles. It was recruited in New York City and consisted of men—mostly German immigrants—from New York City, New Jersey, Maryland and Pennsylvania. It mustered for service in New York during the month of August 1862.[461]

Robert and Paul von König both enlisted in the 68th New York Infantry on August 10, 1861. Paul mustered in as first sergeant of Company F and was promoted to second lieutenant of Company G two days later. On January 17, 1862, he was promoted again, this time to first lieutenant. As a result of his prior military service, Robert was immediately commissioned captain of Company F.[462] The 68th New York was assigned to serve in Major General John C. Frémont's Mountain Department, operating in the Shenandoah Valley of Virginia. The regiment participated in the Battle of Cross Keys on June 8, 1862, during Jackson's Valley Campaign. After Frémont's command was consolidated with the separate commands of Major General Nathaniel Banks and Major General James Shields to form the Army of Virginia under command of Major General John Pope after the end of Jackson's campaign, the 68th New York served in the corps of Major General Franz Sigel, a politically influential German immigrant.

Paul von König was brave and popular with the men under his command. He reminded one officer "of a game cock forgetting all danger in the presence of enemies on the field of battle." Another recalled him "as being inspired to personal deeds of valor in the time of battle, forgetting personal safety even beyond good judgment."[463] He quickly developed a reputation for fearlessness. "He was among the most devoted and audacious scouts," remembered Paul's older brother Friedrich Wilhelm years later. "I still have an authentic order of General Siegel [*sic*], who ordered Paul to make a long-range reconnaissance with 150 cavalrymen."[464] On another occasion, Paul led a detail of 12 enlisted men nearly forty-five miles behind enemy lines to near Culpeper Court House, Virginia, taking 2 prisoners and safely returning despite passing by a village occupied by 1,000 armed Confederate troops.[465]

The 68th New York served throughout Pope's unsuccessful campaign in Virginia that summer, culminating with the disastrous defeat of Pope's army at the Second Battle of Bull Run on August 29–30, 1862. Paul had three horses shot out from under him at Second Bull Run, but the fearless baron never flinched and was not harmed himself.[466]

In recognition of that indomitable courage, Paul received a promotion to captain of Company D on September 22, 1862. However, he did not take command of his company because he was instead detailed to serve on the staff of Major General Carl Schurz, another politically influential German immigrant who had been a leader of the failed Baden Revolution of 1848. Schurz commanded a division in Sigel's corps.[467]

Paul and Robert both spent most of the fall of 1862 on duty in Washington, D.C. While there, they made the acquaintance of Brigadier General James Garfield of Ohio. The future president of the United States was in Washington to serve on the court-martial panel of Major General Fitz-John Porter, accused of insubordination by John Pope. They quickly became fast friends. Garfield described Paul as "a perfect, jolly devil-may-care sort of fellow." Garfield reported to his wife, "Paul von Koenig, the elder, has taken quite a fancy to me and wants to be on my staff if I go to the West."[468] The two officers enjoyed each other's company throughout Paul's stay in Washington, D.C.

While enjoying his stay in Washington, Paul met secretary of the treasury Salmon P. Chase and his beautiful daughter, Kate, next to whom Paul sat at a dinner. When the dashing baron took off his gloves, his rough hands shocked her. She burst out, "But Baron von König what hands you have!" He shot back, "That is from labor," prompting her to blush and respond, "That is most honorable." Such was the company that Paul's contacts and noble pedigree enabled him to keep.[469]

On December 24, 1862, Paul's younger brother Robert resigned his commission and was discharged from the army.[470] Robert apparently returned to Germany after leaving the army, leaving Paul alone in America.[471] The circumstances of Robert's resignation and discharge are not known but presumably had something to do with the lingering effects of his Solferino wound. Robert's adventure in America ended quietly.

Unfortunately, Paul did not get his wish. When Garfield was ordered to join Major General William S. Rosecrans's Army of the Cumberland as chief of staff, von König did not accompany him. At first, he returned to Schurz's staff as the ordnance officer for Schurz's division, but in April 1863, he was assigned to serve on Brigadier General William Woods Averell's staff as an aide de camp and accompanied Averell on the Stoneman Raid. When Averell was relieved of command of his Second Cavalry Division and was reassigned to Wheeling, von König accompanied him. He served with Averell for the rest of his life.[472]

The regimental historian of the 14th Pennsylvania Cavalry, who met the baron when Averell took command of the Fourth Separate Brigade, recalled him as "a brave, dashing cavalryman who knew no fear, whose ambition was to be braver than the bravest of the brave men in General Averell's Division of the Army of West Virginia."[473] It comes as no surprise, then, that Averell gave the baron the most difficult assignments scouting and leading detachments of men into dangerous situations, just as he did at White Sulphur Springs.

Lieutenant John Rodgers Meigs joined Averell's staff on August 12, 1863, just two weeks before Paul von König's death. "He is a very fine soldier and a friend and admirer of Sec. Chase," reported Lieutenant Meigs in a letter to his father on August 23, 1863. Meigs also described the German baron as "a jolly Dutchman" in his letter home.[474]

Paul von König was killed instantly while leading the flank attack of the 14th Pennsylvania Cavalry late on the afternoon of August 26, 1863. Averell singled out the dead hero for special praise when he penned his report of the action, noting his gallantry in action.[475] Circumstances forced Averell to leave his dead behind when he withdrew on August 27. The Confederates buried the dead where they fell on the battlefield, including von König.[476]

Thirty-five years later, in 1898, Captain Thomas R. Kerr of the 14th Pennsylvania Cavalry set out to find the baron's resting place. While he was able to locate the Union and Confederate lines of battle, he failed to find any trace of the grave and gave up. Ten years later, in 1908, Colonel James M. Schoonmaker of the 14th Pennsylvania Cavalry, then the wealthy and prominent president of a railroad, located the house used as a hospital where von König's body was taken. The owner of the house—a Confederate veteran of the Battle of White Sulphur Springs—had helped to bury the dead and remembered "where a German with long hair found at the rock had been buried and took Schoonmaker to the spot, just a short distance below where he had fallen." Schoonmaker made note of the location of the grave.[477]

In 1913, Schoonmaker visited Europe. While there, he met Paul von König's youngest brother, Friedrich Wilhelm Ulrich Götz Freiherr von

A portrait of Lieutenant General Götz von König, painted in 1915 by his son, Leo Freiherr Von König. *Dominik von König.*

König, who was by then a sixty-four-year-old lieutenant general of cavalry in Kaiser Wilhelm II's Landwehr.[478] When Schoonmaker told the general that the long-lost grave of his brother had only recently been located, General von König expressed the hope that the United States government would properly mark the resting place of the lamented hero.[479]

Schoonmaker resolved to erect a suitable marker on the grave of the brave staff officer who died leading a hopeless attack in an attempt to turn defeat into victory. He paid for the monument out of his own pocket and stated that he had done so at the specific request of his younger brother, the lieutenant general.[480] The handsome granite shaft was placed on Paul von König's resting place. A bronze plaque tops it that reads:

Monument to Captain Paul Freiherr von König. *Author photo.*

Baron
Paul von König
Captain U.S.A.
Killed
Aug. 26th, 1863

Along with other veterans of the 14th Pennsylvania Cavalry, Schoonmaker dedicated the monument on November 9, 1914, just over half a century after the baron fell.[481] Unfortunately, his brother, Lieutenant General Götz Freiherr von König, could not attend—World War I was already underway, and the general, as so many other members of the family von König had done over the years, had answered the call of duty and was serving the Fatherland on the eastern front.

The land where the monument stands was sold and developed into a strip shopping center. The monument now rests just outside a Hardee's fast-food restaurant located on an outparcel of the shopping center. It gets little visitation other than from curious diners, but it still stands as a silent sentinel commemorating the life and heroic death of Captain Paul Freiherr von König. The location of his remains is unknown but is presumably somewhere beneath the strip shopping center or its parking lot.

Notes

Introduction

1. A detailed discussion of the history of the formation of the state of West Virginia is beyond the scope of this study. For a detailed discussion, see Rice and Brown, *West Virginia*, 111–23.
2. Ibid., 147.
3. However, some would not be freed until reaching the age of twenty-five under these formulas.
4. Rice and Brown, *West Virginia*, 147.
5. Ibid., 140–50.
6. Ibid., 150–51.
7. Obviously, the details of the Jones-Imboden Raid stray far beyond the scope of this book. For a detailed discussion of the Raid, the only monograph devoted to it is Collins, *Jones-Imboden Raid.*
8. Williams, *West Virginia*, 68.
9. Rice, *History of Greenbrier County*, 261.
10. McKinney, *Civil War in Greenbrier County*, xiii.
11. For the most detailed description of the Battle of Lewisburg, see McKinney, *Civil War in Greenbrier County*, 169–96.
12. Cole, *History of Greenbrier County*, 24.
13. Rice, *History of Greenbrier County*, 283.

Chapter 1

14. Bates, *Martial Deeds*, 849.
15. Reader, *Fifth West Virginia Cavalry*, 197.
16. Warner, *Generals in Blue*, 12–13.
17. Eckert and Amato, *Ten Years in the Saddle*, 388.
18. Collins, *Averell's Salem Raid*, 9.
19. Bates, *Martial Deeds of Pennsylvania*, 850.
20. Collins, *Averell's Salem Raid*, 5.
21. Rhodes, *Cavalry of the Army of the Potomac*.
22. *War of the Rebellion*, series 1, vol. 21, 900 (hereafter cited as *OR*; all further references are to series 1, unless otherwise noted); *Charleston Mercury*, January 5, 1863.
23. *OR*, vol. 21, 895–96, 902.
24. James K. Kim to William W. Averell, February 3, 1863, William Woods Averell Papers, New York State Library and Archives, Albany.
25. William Redwood Price to Averell, February 19, 1863, Averell Papers.
26. For a detailed discussion of the formation of the Army of the Potomac's Cavalry Corps and of these actions, see Wittenberg, *Union Cavalry Comes of Age*.
27. *OR*, vol. 25, part 1, 1072–73.
28. Joseph Hooker to Samuel P. Bates, April 2, 1877, Samuel P. Bates Papers, Pennsylvania State Archives, Harrisburg, Pennsylvania.
29. Doster, *Lincoln and Episodes of the Civil War*, 200–01.
30. Note of the Adjutant General of the Army, May 7, 1863, William Woods Averell file, Letters Received by the Appointment, Commission and Personal Branch of the Adjutant General's Office, 1871–1894, M1395, National Archives, Washington, D.C.
31. William Woods Averell diary, entries for May 14 and May 17, 1863, Averell Papers.
32. *OR*, vol. 25, part 1, 1076–77. Averell wrote, "The form and tenor of the order and its mode of communication are extraordinary. No cause is or has been assigned for its issue, to my knowledge. Issued at the close of the unsuccessful engagement of Sunday, May 3, and destitute of history or explanation, its effect is to place upon me, by implication, an indefinite share in the responsibility for whatever there may have been of failure in the operations of the Army of the Potomac in the recent attack upon

the enemy's forces. I therefore deem it my duty to make you acquainted with the history of the recent cavalry operations in which I took part, to ask your consideration of the inclosed orders, marked A, B, C, D, and E, which controlled my conduct, and to ask that an inquiry be made as to the causes for my removal, and that I may be informed of their nature." Averell continued, "If the execution of my orders was faulty, it cannot be attributed to a misunderstanding of them, as the cavalry, in their recent operations, were engaged in carrying out a part of the plan originated by myself previous to the first battle of Fredericksburg, and which I once set out to execute about the beginning of the year. The major-general commanding the Army of the Potomac also did me the honor to invite my opinion upon the details of these operations before they were ordered, and I believe I thoroughly understood the project of the general commanding, so far as the cavalry was concerned."

33. Hardaway, *On Our Own Soil*, 85.
34. West, *Remember Me*, 212.
35. Lang, *Loyal West Virginia*, 108.
36. Reader, *Fifth West Virginia Cavalry*, 197.
37. Lang, *Loyal West Virginia*, 108.
38. According to historian Terry Lowry, Gibson's Battalion consisted of four companies of West Virginia cavalry, Company C of the 16th Illinois Cavalry and the 3rd Independent Company Ohio Cavalry. See Lowry, *Last Sleep*, 11.
39. *OR*, vol. 29, part 1, 37. Averell stated in his report of the raid that "I did not have 1300 men in the front on the first day" of the Battle of White Sulphur Springs. This number likely reflects attrition from the long marches of July and August 1863.
40. Reader, *Fifth West Virginia Cavalry*, 200.
41. West, *Remember Me*, 212.
42. OR, vol. 27, part 2, 206.
43. Ibid.
44. Lang, *Loyal West Virginia*, 207; Biographical Register of the United States Congress, 1774–Present, http://bioguide.congress.gov/scripts/biodisplay.pl?index=L000107.
45. Lang, *Loyal West Virginia*, 213.
46. Hunt, *Colonels in Blue*, 194.
47. Wiley, *History of Monongalia County*, 529–31.

48. Lang, *Loyal West Virginia*, 217–22.
49. Baumgartner, *First Families of Huntington*, 37–38; Obituary of John H. Oley, *Huntington Advertiser*, March 17, 1888; Hunt and Brown, *Brevet Brigadier*, 454.
50. Lang, *Loyal West Virginia*, 226–27.
51. Emerson, *Col. J.M. Schoonmaker*, 21.
52. *National Tribune*, "General James M. Schoonmaker."
53. Westnam, "The Fourteenth Cavalry."
54. *National Tribune*, "General James M. Schoonmaker."
55. Slease, *14th Pennsylvania Cavalry*, 15–18.
56. Davis, "At Rocky Gap, W. Va."
57. Lowry, *Last Sleep*, 21–23.
58. Reader, *Fifth West Virginia Cavalry*, 69; Lowry, *Last Sleep*, 22.
59. Reid, *Ohio in the War*, 2:929.
60. Lowry, *Last Sleep*, 22.
61. Reader, *Fifth West Virginia Cavalry*, 86–87; Lowry, *Last Sleep*, 29.
62. Thomas, *Round Ball to Rimfire*, 2:137. Approximately 252 of the 501 Lindner carbines were issued to the 8th West Virginia in June 1863. The weapon later proved to be unsatisfactory, and the War Department rejected a shipment of six thousand of them in May 1865. McAulay, *Carbines of the U.S. Cavalry*, 23–24.
63. *OR*, vol. 27, part 2, 209.
64. Slease, *14th Pennsylvania Volunteer Cavalry*, 83–84.
65. Price, "Plain Tales of Mountain Trails," 390.
66. *OR*, vol. 27, part 2, 210–11; Slease, *14th Pennsylvania Volunteer Cavalry*, 85.
67. *OR*, vol. 27, part 2, 211.

CHAPTER 2

68. Slease, *14th Pennsylvania Volunteer Cavalry*, 89.
69. *OR*, vol. 29, part 1, 33.
70. Ibid.
71. Ibid., 38.
72. Ibid., 38–39.
73. Ibid., 39.
74. Giunta, *Civil War Soldier of Christ and Country*, 192.

75. *OR*, vol. 29, part 1, 39–40.
76. Ibid., 40.
77. Ibid., 33.
78. Mathers, "The War in West Virginia."
79. Lyda, "Gen. Averill's Brigade."
80. Slease, *14th Pennsylvania Volunteer Cavalry*, 102.
81. Mathers, "The War in West Virginia."
82. *OR*, vol. 29, part 1, 33.
83. Croft, "Averell's Queer Skirmish at Rocky Gap."
84. *OR*, vol. 29, part 1, 33.
85. Slease, *14thPennsylvania Volunteer Cavalry*, 89.
86. Giunta, *Civil War Soldier of Christ and Country*, 190.
87. Ibid.
88. Ibid.
89. Slease, *14th Pennsylvania Volunteer Cavalry*, 89.
90. Lyda, "General Averill's Brigade."
91. *Richmond Daily Dispatch*, August 22, 1863.
92. Lyda, "General Averill's Brigade."
93. *OR*, vol. 29, part 1, 33.
94. Slease, *14th Pennsylvania Volunteer Cavalry*, 89.
95. Lyda, "General Averill's Brigade."
96. Mathers, "The War in West Virginia."
97. Ibid.
98. *OR*, vol. 29, part 1, 33.
99. Collins, *General William Averell's Salem Raid*, 86.
100. McNeel, "The Imboden Raid and Its Effects," 303.
101. Warner, *Generals in Gray*, 153–54. Mudwall Jackson served one term as lieutenant governor of Virginia prior to the war. He resigned as judge of the nineteenth judicial circuit in 1861, enlisted in the Confederate army as a private and quickly rose to the colonelcy of the 31st Virginia Infantry. In April 1863, he recruited the 19th Virginia Cavalry within the Federal lines in western Virginia and was commissioned its colonel.
102. Jones, "Battle of Dry Creek."
103. *OR*, vol. 29, part 2, 634.
104. Hardaway, *On Our Own Soil*, 65.
105. Ibid., 88.
106. Edgar, "History of the Battle of White Sulphur Springs," 1.

107. Price, "Plain Tales of Mountain Trails," 391–92.
108. *OR*, vol. 29, part 1, 33–34.
109. Lyda, "General Averill's Brigade."
110. *OR*, vol. 29, part 1, 34.
111. Lyda, "General Averill's Brigade."
112. Giunta, *Civil War Soldier of Christ and Country*, 191.
113. *OR*, vol. 29, part 1, 49.
114. West, *Remember Me*, 229.
115. Price, "Plain Tales of Mountain Trails," 392.
116. *OR*, vol. 29, part 1, 34.
117. Giunta, *Civil War Soldier of Christ and Country*, 191.
118. John H. Oley to Capt. Fred Trowbridge, September 1, 1863, William Woods Averell Papers, Special Collections, Honnold/Mudd Library, Claremont College, Claremont, California.
119. *OR*, vol. 29, part 1, 3492.
120. Slease, *14th Pennsylvania Volunteer Cavalry*, 89.
121. Mowrer, *History of the Organization and Service*, 8.
122. Hedgeman Slack to his sister, September 5, 1863, Charles N. Slack collection, Charleston, West Virginia.
123. Samuel B. Knox, letter of June 19, 1899, published in an unidentified newspaper as "No. 16."
124. Reader, *Fifth West Virginia Cavalry*, 203.
125. Oley to Trowbridge, September 21, 1863.
126. *OR*, vol. 29, part 1, 3493.
127. Slease, *14th Pennsylvania Volunteer Cavalry*, 89.
128. Lyda, "General Averill's Brigade."
129. West, *Remember Me*, 229.
130. Slease, *14th Pennsylvania Volunteer Cavalry*, 90.
131. *OR*, vol. 29, part 1, 3494.
132. Reader, *Fifth West Virginia Cavalry*, 203.
133. Lyda, "General Averill's Brigade."
134. *OR*, vol. 29, part 1, 49.
135. Edgar, "The Battle of White Sulphur Springs," 2.
136. Giunta, *Civil War Soldier of Christ and Country*, 191.
137. Ibid. Lieutenant Meigs also made some prescient observations to his father. "We either capture or clear the country west of our line of march of *rebels forces* it will be a pity to abandon it again to be occupied

by a force of 8 or 10 thousand as it has been while we watch along the B&O RR with 30,000. To hold it we would have to occupy each gap with some block houses and field works. The block houses only need to be garrisoned except on approach of the enemy. We could thus with a very small force hold the line of the Alleghanys as far as Lewisburg. Then we would strike westward to the Big Sandy. This line would be as easy to defend as the Alleghany but then we would have no large force in front from which detachments can be sent in quiet times to worry us." Ibid., 191–92, 195.

138. The town of Callaghan is located five miles east of Covington and fifteen miles east of White Sulphur Springs on the James and Kanawha Turnpike. The town was named for the Callaghan Tavern, opened in 1792 by Revolutionary War veteran Dennis Callaghan. It was an important crossroads, and the Callaghan Tavern was a well-known landmark.
139. *OR*, vol. 29, part 1, 34.
140. Mathers, "The War in West Virginia."
141. Lyda, "General Averill's Brigade."
142. Mathers, "The War in West Virginia."

CHAPTER 3

143. *OR*, vol. 29, part 2, 634.
144. Ibid., 652–53.
145. Stevens, "Battle of Dry Creek."6
146. *Richmond Daily Dispatch*, August 27, 1863.
147. *OR*, vol. 29, part 1, 44.
148. MacCorkle, *White Sulphur Springs*, 264.
149. Stevens, "Battle of Dry Creek."
150. Jones, "Foreword," in Jones, *Siege of Charleston*, 5–6.
151. Jones, "Holding Burnside in Check in East Tennessee," in Cozzens, *Battles and Leaders*, 430–31.
152. Robertson, *Soldier of Southwestern Virginia*, 144.
153. Ibid., 157.
154. Davis, *Confederate General*, 2: 92–93.
155. Edgar Papers, Southern Historical Collections.
156. Patton, *The Pattons*, 47.

157. Ibid., 40–41.
158. Brager, "Like His More Famous Namesake," 12, 14.
159. Colonel Isaac W. Patton commanded the 22nd Louisiana Infantry. Colonel Tazewell Waller Patton commanded the 13th Virginia Infantry and was mortally wounded while leading his regiment during Pickett's Charge at Gettysburg on July 3, 1863. Colonel John Mercer Patton Jr. briefly commanded the 21st Virginia Infantry and then served as a judge advocate officer. See Allardice, *Confederate Colonels*, 300–01. Two other brothers also served in the Confederate army.
160. Hayden, *Virginia Genealogies*, 33.
161. Lowry, *Last Sleep*, 40.
162. Faulkner, *Dear Annie*, 28.
163. Lowry, *22nd Virginia Infantry*, dust jacket.
164. Derrick obituary, *National Intelligencer*, May 17, 1852.
165. One source states that Derrick was dismissed from the army on July 16, 1861, for tendering his resignation in the face of the enemy. See Kirshner, *Class of 1861*, 79.
166. Anderson, *Sharples-Sharpless Family*, 1:326; Krick, *Lee's Colonels*, 118.
167. Lowry, *Last Sleep*, 43.
168. Ibid., 44.
169. Walls, "A History of the White Sulphur Rifles," 17–18.
170. Lowry, *Last Sleep*, 44.
171. Ibid., 45.
172. Ibid.
173. Scott, *45th Virginia Infantry*, 2–3.
174. Morrison, *Memoirs of Henry Heth*, 152.
175. Scott, *45th Virginia Infantry*, 25–30.
176. Allardice, *Confederate Colonels*, 80.
177. Johnston, *Captain Beirne Chapman*, 1–6.
178. Ibid.
179. *OR*, vol. 29, part 2, 663.
180. Ibid., 664.
181. Ibid., part 1, 44, 42.
182. Ibid., part 2, 666. He sent very similar orders to the Home Guard commander at Salem, also instructing those troops to be prepared to move at a moment's notice to defend the New River Bridge. Ibid., 668.
183. Robertson, *Soldier of Southwestern Virginia*, 180.

184. *OR*, vol. 29, part 1, 44.
185. *Richmond Daily Dispatch*, August 28, 1863.
186. *OR*, vol. 29, part 1, 45.
187. Arbogast, "The Battle of Dry Creek," 14.
188. *Richmond Daily Dispatch*, August 28, 1863.
189. Edgar, "The Battle of White Sulphur Springs," 2.
190. *Richmond Daily Dispatch*, August 26, 1863.
191. Price, "Plain Tales of Mountain Trails," 393.
192. *OR*, vol. 29, part 1, 45. Jackson later claimed that "when I first arrived at Gatewood's and on several occasions, I dispatched to Colonel Patton (with the request that he forward to the general commanding) my opinion that the enemy would, after driving my command out of the way, proceed to Lewisburg, and I also dispatched to him, with the same request, all my movements until after I had fallen back from Warm Springs." Ibid., 52. Patton never mentioned these dispatches in his report, so it is likely that they were not received. If Jackson indeed sent these dispatches, he had divined Averell's intentions. Undoubtedly such intelligence would have been important to Jones's and Patton's planning for responding to the threat posed by Averell's invading force.
193. Edgar, "Battle of White Sulphur Springs," 2.
194. Henry C. Carpenter to "My Dear Sister Emily," September 4, 1863, Special Collections, Virginia Polytechnic Institute, Blacksburg, Virginia.
195. Humphreys, "Personal Reminiscences of the Battle of Dry Creek."
196. MacCorkle, *White Sulphur Springs*, 265–66.

Chapter 4

197. McNeel, "Battle of Dry Creek."
198. *OR*, vol. 29, part 1, 34–35.
199. Mathers, "The War in West Virginia."
200. Reader, *Fifth West Virginia Cavalry*, 119.
201. *OR*, vol. 29, part 1, 35.
202. Ibid., 60.
203. Edgar, "Battle of White Sulphur Springs," 2.
204. Humphreys, "Personal Reminiscences of the Battle of Dry Creek."
205. *OR*, vol. 29, part 1, 55. Branham was actually a member of Brigadier

General John Echols's staff, but he had been serving with Patton since Echols had to take sick leave. Patton praised Branham's energy, skill and courage in his after-action report of the battle.

206. Reader, *Fifth West Virginia Cavalry*, 204.
207. Groft, "Averell's Queer Skirmish at Rocky Gap."
208. George M. Edgar to Francis H. Smith, August 31, 1863, Superintendent's Records, Incoming Correspondence, Archives, Virginia Military Institute, Lexington, Virginia.
209. *OR*, vol. 29, part 1, 53.
210. Humphreys, "Personal Reminiscences of the Battle of Dry Creek."
211. Noyes, "Reminiscences of the Battle of Dry Creek."
212. Stevens, "Battle of Dry Creek."
213. *OR*, vol. 29, part 1, 65.
214. Stevens, "Battle of Dry Creek."
215. Humphreys, "Personal Reminiscences of the Battle of Dry Creek."
216. *OR*, vol. 29, part 1, 53.
217. Ibid., 58.
218. Ibid., 62.
219. Knox, "Battle of Rocky Gap."
220. Mathers, "War in West Virginia."
221. Lyda, "Gen. Averill's Brigade."
222. Ibid.
223. Brian Stuart Kesterson to the author, June 10, 2010.
224. *OR*, vol. 29, part 1, 35. It is important to note that when cavalry fights dismounted, its effective strength is automatically reduced by 25 percent, since one out of every four men has the task of holding his horse and those of three others at the ready, so that the riders can quickly mount up and move out as needed. This means that if Averell deployed his entire brigade in a dismounted fight, he would have fewer than one thousand carbines on the line of battle.
225. Ibid., 65.
226. Lyda, "Gen. Averill's Brigade."
227. Oley to Trowbridge, September 1, 1863.
228. Benjamin Ronk diary, entry for August 26, 1863, West Virginia State Archives, Charleston, West Virginia.
229. *Gallipolis Journal*, September 17, 1863.
230. Ibid., September 3, 1863.

231. Oley to Trowbridge, September 1, 1863.
232. Ibid.
233. *OR*, vol. 29, part 1, 35.
234. Ibid.
235. Mowrer, *History of the Organization and Service*, 8.
236. Affidavit of William Woods Averell of February 6, 1893, Chatham T. Ewing pension file, RG 94, NARA. Ewing died in July 1892 from a gunshot wound to the abdomen received at White Sulphur Springs that resulted in a disease of the bowels. Averell later stated that he believed that Ewing's wounds contributed to his early death. Ibid.
237. Affidavit of Adam Brown, July 16, 1889, Ewing pension file.
238. Reader, *Fifth West Virginia Cavalry*, 204.
239. Mowrer, *History of the Organization and Service*, 65.
240. Johnson, "The Battle of Dry Creek."
241. Johnston, *Captain Beirne Chapman*, 77.
242. Slease, *14th Pennsylvania Volunteer Cavalry*, 90–91.
243. *OR*, vol. 29, part 1, 35.
244. Groft, "Averell's Queer Skirmish at Rocky Gap."
245. Reader, *Fifth West Virginia Cavalry*, 120.
246. Slease, *14th Pennsylvania Volunteer Cavalry*, 90.
247. *OR*, vol. 29, part 1, 58.
248. Ibid., 53.
249. Parke, "F.J. Parke on Dry Creek Field."
250. Humphreys, "Personal Reminiscences of the Battle of Dry Creek."
251. Scott, *45th Virginia Infantry*, 30.
252. *OR*, vol. 29, part 1, 62.
253. Ibid., 60–61.
254. Rand, "Reminiscences of the Battle of Dry Creek."
255. *OR*, vol. 29, part 1, 62–63.
256. Humphreys, "Personal Reminiscences of the Battle of Dry Creek."
257. Crayon, "Recollections of Civil War Days in Greenbrier."
258. *OR*, vol. 29, part 1, 53.
259. Stevens, "Battle of Dry Creek."
260. Reader, *Fifth West Virginia Cavalry*, 205.
261. *OR*, vol. 29, part 1, 64.
262. Ibid., 35–36.
263. Reader, *Fifth West Virginia Cavalry*, 76.

264. *OR*, vol. 29, part 1, 53–54. Barbee's wound was so severe that he was unable to return to active duty in the field with the regiment. Lowry, *22nd Virginia Infantry*, 46. In December 1863, Barbee wrote to his wife: "My wounds have entirely healed. While East a large piece of bone worked out near right elbow joint from which again followed an Erysipelatous inflammation & gave me much pain. All however is now well. I sometimes suffer pain about my left hip where I was beaten with a gun. Sometimes I fear the heavy blows recd on crest of Ischium will yet bring about Caries of that part of the bone." He indicated that he soon expected to regain full use of the wounded arm and returned to duty in the winter of 1864. Andrew R. Barbee to his wife, December 7, 1863, Letters Received 1863–1865, Department of West Virginia, Entry 5691, RG 393, U.S. Army Continental Commands 1821–1920, NARA. When he returned to duty, Barbee did not return to the 22nd Virginia. Instead, he was assigned to duty in the Confederate medical department and served out the rest of the war in that capacity. Miller and Maxwell, *West Virginia and Its People*, 2:202.

265. *OR*, vol. 29, part 1, 58.

266. Ibid.

267. Mathers, "The War in West Virginia."

268. George S. Patton to C.Q. Tompkins, September 27, 1863, Terry Lowry collection, Charleston, West Virginia.

269. Benjamin, "Killed in Battle with Four Names."

270. *OR*, vol. 29, part 1, 54.

271. Stevens, "Battle of Dry Creek."

272. Humphreys, "Personal Reminiscences of the Battle of Dry Creek."

273. *OR*, vol. 29, part 2, 60.

274. Ibid., 54.

275. Ibid., 60.

276. Stevens, "Battle of Dry Creek."

277. MacCorkle, *White Sulphur Springs*, 268.

278. Stevens, "Battle of Dry Creek."

279. Lowry, *22nd Virginia Infantry*, 47.

280. *OR*, vol. 29, part 1, 36.

CHAPTER 5

281. *OR*, vol. 29, part 1, 36.
282. Ibid., 61.
283. Reader, *Fifth West Virginia Cavalry*, 205.
284. *OR*, vol. 29, part 1, 36.
285. Ibid., 38.
286. Ibid., 54.
287. Ibid., 61.
288. Slease, *14th Pennsylvania Volunteer Cavalry*, 91.
289. James McChesney to his sister, September 4, 1863, H.E. Matheny collection, Akron, Ohio.
290. Slease, *14th Pennsylvania Volunteer Cavalry*, 91.
291. Ibid., 248.
292. Stevens, "The Battle of Dry Creek."
293. Ibid.
294. MacCorkle, *White Sulphur Springs*, 269.
295. Charles Mestrezat to his wife, undated letter, Charles Mestrezat letters, Special Collections, West Virginia University, Morgantown, West Virginia.
296. Edgar, "The Battle of White Sulphur Springs," 7.
297. *OR*, vol. 29, part 1, 38.
298. Groft, "Averell's Queer Skirmish at Rocky Gap." Sergeant Joshua Groft of the 14th Pennsylvania did not care for the baron, whom he described as "a very overbearing officer." Groft later recounted that "they say he was killed by our own men, for he was found shot in the back." There is no evidence to suggest that von König was shot by anyone other than one of Patton's foot soldiers. Sergeant Groft's claim that his own men killed Captain von König cannot be corroborated and should be discounted. A member of the 3rd West Virginia claimed that von König was intoxicated. "He was under the influence of liquor and approached our Colonel on the field, inquired for the 8th [West] Virginia, was told not to go in that direction he was then taking or he would be shot. He persisted and fell in sight of several of our men," he claimed. Lyda, "General Averill's Brigade." There is also nothing to corroborate the claim that Baron von König was intoxicated either.
299. Slease, *14th Pennsylvania Volunteer Cavalry*, 92.
300. *OR*, vol. 29, part 1, 36.

301. Slease, *14th Pennsylvania Volunteer Cavalry*, 91; Reader, *Fifth West Virginia Cavalry*, 206.
302. Reader, *Fifth West Virginia Cavalry*, 34.
303. *OR*, vol. 29, part 1, 64; Reader, *Fifth West Virginia Cavalry*, 205.
304. Reader, *Fifth West Virginia Cavalry*, 205.
305. *OR*, vol. 29, part 1, 59.
306. Ibid., 36; Reader, *Fifth West Virginia Cavalry*, 205.
307. Groft, "Averell's Queer Skirmish at Rocky Gap."
308. *OR*, vol. 29, part 1, 54.
309. Carpenter to his sister, September 4, 1863.
310. *OR*, vol. 29, part 1, 59. Upon learning of her husband's death after the battle, Mrs. traveled to West Virginia to try to reclaim her late husband's remains. She spent three traumatic weeks in Beverly in the hope of getting a pass to go through the lines to retrieve her husband's remains. Collins, *General William Averell's Salem Raid*, 34.
311. *OR*, vol. 29, part 1, 54.
312. Scott, *45th Virginia Infantry*, 30.
313. *OR*, vol. 29, part 1, 63.
314. Scott, *45th Virginia Infantry*, 30.
315. Reader, *Fifth West Virginia Cavalry*, 206.
316. Lyda, "Gen. Averill's Brigade."
317. *OR*, vol. 29, part 1, 54.
318. Groft, "Averell's Queer Skirmish at Rocky Gap"; *OR*, vol. 29, part 1, 61.
319. Johnston, *Captain Beirne Chapman and Chapman's Battery*, 14.
320. Groft, "Averell's Queer Skirmish at Rocky Gap."
321. Mathers, "The War in West Virginia."
322. Lyda, "General Averill's Brigade."
323. McNeel, "Battle of Dry Creek."
324. *OR*, vol. 29, part 1, 3699.
325. Ibid., 54.
326. Oley to Townsend, September 1, 1863.
327. Mathers, "The War in West Virginia."
328. Slease, *14th Pennsylvania Volunteer Cavalry*, 92.
329. Ibid.
330. *OR*, vol. 29, part 1, 45.
331. Jones, "Battle of Dry Creek."

332. *OR*, vol. 29, part 1, 36.
333. Stevens, "Reminiscences of the Battle of Dry Creek."
334. *OR*, vol. 29, part 1, 36.
335. Groft, "Averell's Queer Skirmish at Rocky Gap."
336. *OR*, vol. 29, part 1, 59.
337. Ibid., 63.
338. Ibid., 55.
339. Ibid., 56.
340. Patton, *The Pattons*, 48. Shortly after his eleventh birthday, George William Patton changed his name to George Smith Patton to honor his father, who was killed in action at the Third Battle of Winchester on September 19, 1864. That's why his son was named George Smith Patton Jr., who became a legendary hero of World War II.
341. Robertson, *Soldier of Southwestern Virginia*, 180; Weaver, *Virginia Home Guards*, 134–35.
342. *OR*, vol. 29, part 1, 43 and 45. Jones wrote in his report, "If Wharton's brigade had moved by railroad to Millborough, as I supposed it would, it would have reached Callaghan's on the evening of the 26th or morning of the 27th. With that force at Callaghan's and the First Brigade pressing in the rear, the country is such that I scarcely think that General Averell's command could have escaped destruction." Ibid., 45.
343. Ibid., 50.

Chapter 6

344. *OR*, vol. 29, part 1, 36–37.
345. For a detailed discussion of the Battle of Kelly's Ford, see Wittenberg, *Union Cavalry Comes of Age*, 71–110.
346. Knox, "Ed. Leader," 10.
347. *OR*, vol. 29, part 1, 42.
348. Ibid., 61.
349. Davis, "At Rocky Gap, W. Va."
350. *OR*, vol. 29, part 1, 63.
351. Ibid., 61.
352. Ibid., 31.
353. Ibid., 55.

354. Ibid., 59.
355. Lyda, "General Averill's Brigade."
356. The *Official Records* do not indicate precisely where or what Scammon's troops were doing during the Battle of White Sulphur Springs, but it does not appear that they ever left their base camp near Charleston in the Kanawha River Valley and never made any real effort to come to Averell's assistance. Colonel Rutherford B. Hayes, the future president who commanded one of Scammon's regiments, wrote on August 5, "We shall go up to Lewisburg, I guess, in two or three weeks to see after the Rebels in that quarter." Williams, *Diary and Letters of Rutherford B. Hayes*, 2:428. Hayes continued to send letters home, all of which indicated that the command was still at its base outside Charleston, even after the great law book raid ended.
357. *OR*, vol. 29, part 1, 59.
358. Lyda, "General Averill's Brigade."
359. Reader, *Fifth West Virginia Cavalry*, 206.
360. *OR*, vol. 29, part 1, 59.
361. Knox, "Ed. Leader," 10.
362. Slease, *14th Pennsylvania Volunteer Cavalry*, 93.
363. Mathers, "The War in West Virginia."
364. *OR*, vol. 29, part 1, 61.
365. Ibid., 45.
366. Ibid.
367. Slease, *14th Pennsylvania Cavalry*, 225–26. Wilson was initially imprisoned at Libby Prison and then was transferred to South Carolina. He escaped once and was then imprisoned in Charleston. Along with a lieutenant of a New Jersey regiment, he escaped again but, owing to starvation, was unable to make it out of Charleston. An unknown African American man hid him in his cabin, where Wilson died on November 24, 1864. He was buried in the yard of the cabin and then, after the war, removed to the National Cemetery in Charleston, where he rests today. Ibid., 226.
368. Groft, "Averell's Queer Skirmish at Rocky Gap."
369. Slease, *14th Pennsylvania Cavalry*, 249–50.
370. *OR*, vol. 29, part 1, 55.
371. Ibid., 57.
372. Stevens, "Reminiscences of the Battle of Dry Creek."
373. *OR*, vol. 29, part 2, 677.
374. Ibid., part 1, 46.

375. *Richmond Daily Dispatch*, August 31, 1863.
376. McKinney, *Civil War in Greenbrier County*, 267.
377. James Steel McClung war memoirs, Terry Lowry collection, Charleston, West Virginia.
378. The family cemetery on the grounds of the Greenbrier is difficult to locate, as it is tucked in amongst expensive rental cottages. There are no signs denoting it, and it does not appear on maps of the resort. It took the author and West Virginia historian Terry Lowry nearly an hour of searching to locate the cemetery, even though they had a general idea of where it could be found. The graves overlooking the CSX Railroad (the modern successor to the Virginia Central) tracks are even more remote and are more difficult to locate. There are undoubtedly a good number of battlefield graves that remain undisturbed to this day.
379. Stevens, "Reminiscences of the Battle of Dry Creek."
380. Ibid.
381. Johnson, "The Battle of Dry Creek."
382. *Richmond Daily Dispatch*, September 3, 1863.
383. Ibid., September 4, 1863.

Chapter 7

384. Mathers, "The War in West Virginia."
385. *OR*, vol. 29, part 1, 50–51.
386. Ibid.
387. Carpenter to his sister, September 4, 1863, Carpenter letters.
388. For a detailed biographical sketch of Colonel Corns, see Dickinson, *Wayne County, West Virginia*, 14. Corns was captured in March 1863 and was released from his parole by exchange on June 10, 1863. Ibid.
389. *OR*, vol. 29, part 1, 57.
390. Ibid., 37.
391. Ibid., 57.
392. Ibid., 51.
393. Mathers, "The War in West Virginia."
394. West, *Remember Me*, 231.
395. Reader, *Fifth West Virginia Cavalry*, 206.
396. *OR*, vol. 29, part 1, 51.

397. Thomas M. Harris to William Rumsey, August 28, 1863, William Woods Averell Papers, Honnold/Mudd Library, Claremont College, Claremont, California.
398. Mathers, "The War in West Virginia."
399. *OR*, vol. 29, part 1, 37.
400. Mathers, "The War in West Virginia."
401. Ronk diary, entry for August 31, 1863.
402. *OR*, vol. 29, part 1, 43.
403. Ibid., 52.
404. Ibid., 57.
405. Ibid., 51–52.
406. Ibid., part 2, 680.
407. Ibid. The threat posed by Longstreet's advance on Knoxville was so severe that Robert E. Lee had to detach Lieutenant General James Longstreet and his First Corps of the Army of Northern Virginia to contend with it. While there is no monograph dedicated to the Knoxville Campaign, for the most detailed analysis of it yet published, see Woodworth, *Six Armies in Tennessee.*
408. Slease, *14th Pennsylvania Volunteer Cavalry*, 93.
409. Mathers, "The War in West Virginia."
410. *OR*, vol. 29, part 1, 50.
411. West, *Remember Me*, 231.
412. *OR*, vol. 29, part 1, 37.
413. Oley to Trowbridge, September 1, 1863.
414. *OR*, vol. 29, part 1, 44.
415. Jones, "Holding Burnside in Check," 433.
416. Slease, *14th Pennsylvania Volunteer Cavalry*, 93.
417. *OR*, vol. 29, part 1, 37. During the raid, the Fourth Separate Brigade passed through six West Virginia counties: Randolph, Hardy, Pendleton, Highland, Pocahontas and Greenbrier.

CHAPTER 8

418. Slease, *14th Pennsylvania Volunteer Cavalry*, 94.
419. Mathers, "The War in West Virginia."
420. Lyda, "Gen. Averill's Brigade."
421. Slease, *14th Pennsylvania Volunteer Cavalry*, 94.

422. Edgar, "The Battle of White Sulphur Springs," 1.
423. *OR*, vol. 29, part 1, 41.
424. Ibid., 56. Patton's numbers do not include any losses sustained in the command of Mudwall Jackson.
425. Slease, *14th Pennsylvania Volunteer Cavalry*, 106.
426. Johnston, *Captain Beirne Chapman*, 15.
427. *OR*, vol. 29, part 1, 64.
428. Ibid., 58.
429. *Abingdon Virginian*, September 11, 1863.
430. Fielding R. Cornett to Rosamond Hale, September 5, 1863, Fielding Raphne Cornett Papers, Special Collections, Alderman Library, University of Virginia, Charlottesville, Virginia.
431. *OR*, vol. 29, part 1, 63.
432. Davis and Hoffman, *Confederate General*, 2:93.
433. Quoted in Krick, "The Confederate Pattons," in Gallagher, *Shenandoah Valley Campaign*, 358.
434. Patton, *The Pattons*, 55. It is believed that Patton's promotion to brigadier general was finally approved by the Confederate senate just before the September 1864 Third Battle of Winchester, but the commission did not reach his brigade until shortly after his death.
435. Patton to Tompkins, September 27, 1863.
436. Rosecrans had won the early campaigns in West Virginia involving the Kanawha Division in 1861–62, which led to his promotion to army command. Obviously, the fall of Chattanooga and the subsequent Chickamauga Campaign stray far beyond the boundaries of this study. For the best study of the campaign yet published, see Cozzens, *This Terrible Sound.*
437. Jones, "Holding Burnside in Check," 430.
438. *OR*, vol. 29, part 2, 709.
439. McNeel, "The Imboden Raid and Its Effects," 303.
440. A November 1863 *New York Times* article openly mocked Mudwall Jackson. "He got his title 'Mudwall' from the fact that in all his fights in East Tennessee he ensconced himself in a muddy ditch—the 'last ditch,' we should surmise." It does not appear that the Federals ever gave Jackson much respect after his humiliation at the hands of William Woods Averell in August 1863. *New York Times*, "The Defeat of Mudwall Jackson," November 22, 1863.
441. Mathers, "The War in West Virginia."

442. Lang, *Loyal West Virginia*, 109.
443. Arbogast, "The Battle of Dry Creek," 8. After the end of the Civil War, this law library was, indeed, relocated to Charleston, West Virginia, where it served as the nucleus of the law library for the Supreme Court of West Virginia. Ibid.
444. For an excellent detailed monograph on the Battle of Droop Mountain, see Lowry, *Last Sleep*.
445. Patton, *The Pattons*, 54–55.
446. For the only detailed monograph on the Salem Raid, see Collins, *Averell's Salem Raid*, 102.
447. Slease, *14th Pennsylvania Volunteer Cavalry*, 194.
448. Taylor, *James E. Taylor Sketchbook*, 458.

APPENDIX B

449. Dominik Freiherr von König, "The Family von König."
450. Ibid.
451. Ibid.
452. Dominik Freiherr von König to the author, October 25, 2010.
453. Friedrich Wilhelm Freiherr von König, "Reminiscences of My Life," von König Collection.
454. Ibid.
455. A detailed description of the Second Opium War strays far beyond the scope of this study. The Second Opium War—also known as the Arrow War, for the ship that was sunk to trigger the conflict—pit the British Empire and the Second French Empire against the Chinese Qing Dynasty and was fought over the legalization of the opium trade, expanding coolie trade, opening all of China to British merchants and exempting foreign imports from internal transit duties. For more about the Second Opium War, see Wong, *Deadly Dreams*.
456. New York Civil War Muster Roll Abstracts, Archive Collection #13775-83, Box #271, Roll # 1143-1144, New York State Library and Archives, Cultural Education Center, Albany, New York. For more on the Argentine civil war of 1861, see Levene, *A History of Argentina*.
457. Slease, *14th Pennsylvania Volunteer Cavalry*, 106.
458. Williams, *Wild Life of the Army*, 150.

459. Ibid.
460. Colonel Betge was thirty-seven and had been a stationer and bookseller before the war. He was from Württemberg, Germany. Betge was discharged for disability from rheumatism and "great nervousness" on August 6, 1862. See Hunt, *Colonels in Blue*, 44. In 1864, Prince Felix zu Salm-Salm, a member of the Prussian royal family, assumed command of the 68th New York.
461. Phisterer, *New York in the War of the Rebellion*, 5:2673.
462. Paul von König service records, RG 94, Consolidated Service Records for the 68th New York Volunteer Infantry, National Archives and Records Administration, Washington, D.C.
463. Slease, *14th Pennsylvania Volunteer Cavalry*, 228.
464. von König, "Reminiscences of My Life."
465. Williams, *Wild Life of the Army*, 153.
466. Ibid., 151.
467. Paul von König service records.
468. Williams, *Wild Life of the Army*, 150–51.
469. von König, "Reminiscences of My Life." The original manuscript suggests that Paul met the daughter of John Hay and his daughter, but Hay was only twenty-four years old in the fall of 1862 and was unmarried. The manuscript does indicate that Paul met the secretary of the treasury, Chase, who had a beautiful daughter named Kate, who was married to Governor William Sprague of Rhode Island. The manuscript claims that Paul became engaged to the young woman he met, but there is no corroboration, and Kate Chase was already married.
470. New York Civil War Muster Roll Abstracts, entry for Robert von König.
471. *Annual Report*, 27:1222. According to the current Baron von König, Robert married for the second time in Germany in 1881, and he died in Berlin in December 1816. Dominik Freiherr von König to the author, April 27, 2011.
472. Paul von König service records.
473. Slease, *14th Pennsylvania Volunteer Cavalry*, 228.
474. Giunta, *Civil War Soldier of Christ and Country*, 192.
475. *OR*, vol. 29, part 1, 37.
476. Slease, *14th Pennsylvania Volunteer Cavalry*, 229.
477. Ibid., 230.
478. Götz von König served in the Franco-Prussian War of 1870 and was

the first Kommandeur der 3, Landwehr-Division, and from 1916, was the Führer des Landwehrkorps, fighting in close connection with the Austrian-Hungarian army against the Russian army in the region that is today Belarus. He was awarded the Blue Max, Imperial Germany's highest military honor, on July 23, 1915. Dominik Freiherr von König to the author, April 26, 2011. Götz von König was the last of this renowned military family to serve in the German military. His son, Leo Freiherr von König (1871–1944), became widely known as an artist and especially as a portraitist—a surprising profession in a family where some members still cultivate the soil in the region of Brunswick, which is now in the state of Lower Saxony. Leo Freiherr von König was also a vocal opponent of the Nazi regime.

479. Slease, *14th Pennsylvania Volunteer Cavalry*, 230.

480. Ibid., 106.

481. Ibid., 230–31.

Bibliography

Primary Sources

Newspapers

Abingdon Virginian
Charleston Daily Mail
Charleston Mercury
Cincinnati Gazette
Daily National Republican
Fayette Tribune
Greenbrier Independent
Huntington Advertiser
Ironton Register
Lynchburg Republican
Monroe Watchman [Union, West Virginia]
National Intelligencer
National Tribune
New York Daily Tribune
New York Times
Philadelphia Weekly Times
Pittsburgh Press
Pomeroy Leader

Richmond Daily Dispatch
Wheeling Intelligencer

Manuscript Materials

Averell, William Woods. Papers. New York State Library and Archives, Cultural Education Center, Albany, New York.

———. Papers. Special Collections, Honnold/Mudd Library, Claremont Colleges, Claremont, California.

Bates, Samuel P. Papers. Pennsylvania State Archives, Harrisburg, Pennsylvania.

Carpenter, Henry C. Letters. Special Collections, Virginia Polytechnic Institute, Blacksburg, Virginia.

Cornett, Fielding Raphne. Papers. Special Collections, Alderman Library, University of Virginia, Charlottesville, Virginia.

Edgar, George M. Papers. "History of the Battle of White Sulphur Springs, Dry Creek or Rocky Gap, Aug. 26–27, 1863." Unpublished ms., Folder 17. Southern Historical Collection, Wilson Library, University of North Carolina, Chapel Hill, North Carolina.

McChesney, James. Letter, September 4, 1863. H.E. Matheny Collection, Akron, Ohio.

McClung, James Steel. Memoirs. Terry Lowry Collection, Charleston, West Virginia.

Mestrezat, Charles Alexander. Letters. Special Collections, West Virginia and Regional History Collection, West Virginia University, Morgantown, West Virginia.

National Archives and Records Administration. RG 94, Consolidated Service Records; RG 94, Pension Files; RG 393, Letters Received 1863–1865, Department of West Virginia, U.S. Army Continental Commands 1821–1920; William Woods Averell File, Letters Received by the Appointment, Commission, and Personnel Branch of the Adjutant General's Office, 1871–1894, M1395. Washington, D.C.

New York Civil War Muster Roll Abstracts, Archive Collection #13775-83, Box #271, Roll # 1143-1144. New York State Library and Archives, Cultural Education Center, Albany, New York.

Patton, George, S. Letter, September 27, 1863. Terry Lowry Collection, Charleston, West Virginia.

Polsley, John J. Letters. Special Collections, Bierce Library, University of Akron, Akron, Ohio.

Ronk, Benjamin. Diary. West Virginia State Archives, Charleston, West Virginia.

Slack, Hedgeman. Letters. Charles N. Slack Collection, Charleston, West Virginia.

Superintendent's Records, Incoming Correspondence. Archives, Virginia Military Institute, Lexington, Virginia.

Von König, Dominik Freiherr. "The Family von König." Unpublished ms. Freiherr von König Collection. Polling, Bavaria, Germany.

Von König, Friedrich Wilhelm Freiherr. "Reminiscences of My Life." Unpublished ms. Freiherr von König Collection. Polling, Bavaria, Germany.

Published Materials

Annual Report of the Adjutant General of the State of New York for the Year 1893. 43 vols. Albany: Office of the Adjutant General of the State of New York, 1894.

Crayon, Mark. "Recollections of Civil War Days in Greenbrier." *Fayette Tribune*, February 24, 1926.

Davis, William A.R. "At Rocky Gap, W. Va." *National Tribune*, November 5, 1916.

Doster, William E. *Lincoln and Episodes of the Civil War.* New York: G.P. Putnam's Sons, 1915.

Eckert, Edward K., and Nicholas J. Amato, eds. *Ten Years in the Saddle: The Memoir of William Woods Averell, 1851–1862.* San Rafael, CA: Presidio Press, 1978.

Faulkner, Virginia, ed. *Dear Annie: A Collection of Letters, 1860–1886.* Parsons, WV, 1969.

Giunta, Mary A., ed. *A Civil War Soldier of Christ and Country: The Selected Correspondence of John Rodgers Meigs, 1859–64.* Urbana: University of Illinois Press, 2006.

Groft, Joshua. "Averell's Queer Skirmish at Rocky Gap." *National Tribune*, September 27, 1883.

Humphreys, C.W. "Personal Reminiscences of the Battle of Dry Creek." *Monroe Watchman*, August 25, 1910.

Johnson, J.F. "The Battle of Dry Creek." *Monroe Watchman*, February 10, 1916.

Johnston, Albert S. *Captain Beirne Chapman and Chapman's Battery*. Union, WV: privately published, 1905.

Jones, David C. "Battle of Dry Creek." *Monroe Watchman*, March 19, 1908.

Jones, Emily Read. "Foreword." In Samuel Jones, *The Siege of Charleston and the Operations on the South Atlantic Coast in the War Among the States*. New York: Neale, 1911.

Jones, Samuel. "Holding Burnside in Check in East Tennessee." In *Battles and Leaders of the Civil War*. Vol. 5. Edited by Peter Cozzens. Urbana: University of Illinois Press, 2002.

Lyda, A.J. "Gen. Averill's Brigade—March and Battle at White Sulphur Springs." *Wheeling Intelligencer*, September 9, 1863.

Mathers, Irwin F. "The War in West Virginia." *Cincinnati Gazette*, September 15, 1863.

McNeel, John A. "Battle of Dry Creek." *Monroe Watchman*, August 27, 1908.

———. "The Imboden Raid and Its Effects." *Southern Historical Society Papers* 34 (January–December 1906).

Morrison, James L., Jr., ed. *The Memoirs of Henry Heth*. Santa Barbara, CA: Greenwood Press, 1974.

Mowrer, G.H. *History of the Organization and Service, During the War of the Rebellion, of Co. A, 14th Pennsylvania Cavalry*. N.p., n.d.

National Tribune. "General James M. Schoonmaker: The Brilliant Cavalryman Who Has Become the Head of the Gettysburg Battlefield Commission." April 17, 1913.

Parke, F.J. "F.J. Parke on Dry Creek Field." *Monroe Watchman*, February 24, 1916.

Phisterer, Frederick. *New York in the War of the Rebellion, 1861–1865*. 3rd ed. 6 vols. Albany, NY: J.B. Lyon Co., 1912.

Rand, Noyes. "Reminiscences of the Battle of Dry Creek on August 26–27, 1863." *Monroe Watchman*, July 8, 1909.

Reader, Francis Smith. *History of the Fifth West Virginia Cavalry, Formerly the Second Virginia, and Battery G First West Virginia Light Artillery*. New Brighton, PA: Daily News, 1890.

Robertson, James I., Jr., ed. *Soldier of Southwestern Virginia: The Civil War Letters of Captain John Preston Sheffey*. Baton Rouge: Louisiana State University Press, 2004.

Slease, William D. *The 14th Pennsylvania Cavalry in the Civil War*. Pittsburgh, PA: Art Engraving and Printing Co., 1890.

Stevens, John G. "Battle of Dry Creek. Confederate Account of the Important Battle of Civil War in Greenbrier County." *Fayette Tribune and Free Press*, January 6, 1916.

Taylor, James E. *The James E. Taylor Sketchbook.* Dayton, OH: Morningside, 1989.

The War of the Rebellion: A Compilation of the Official Records of the Union and Confederate Armies. 128 vols. 3 series. Washington, D.C.: U.S. Government Printing Office, 1889.

West, Alan I., ed. *Remember Me: Civil War Letters Home from a Hospital Steward 1862–1864, Daniel McKinley Martin.* Chicora, PA: Firefly Publications, 2010.

Williams, Charles Richard, ed. *The Diary and Letters of Rutherford B. Hayes, Nineteenth President of the United States.* 5 vols. Columbus: Ohio State Archaeological and Historical Society, 1922.

Williams, Frederick D., ed. *The Wild Life of the Army: Civil War Letters of James A. Garfield.* East Lansing: Michigan State University Press, 1964.

Websites

Biographical Register of the United States Congress, 1774–Present. http://bioguide.congress.gov/scripts/biodisplay.pl?index=L000107.

SECONDARY SOURCES

Articles

Arbogast, John A. "The Battle of Dry Creek." *Journal of the Greenbrier Historical Society* 1, no. 6 (October 1968): 7–23.

Benjamin, J.W. "Killed in Battle with Four Names: Unique Marker Honors Fallen Soldier." *Charleston Daily Mail,* March 3, 1976.

Boehm, Robert B. "The Unfortunate Averell." *Civil War Times Illustrated* 5 (August 1996): 30–36.

Brager, Bruce L. "Like His Famous Namesake, Confederate Colonel George S. Patton Was a Quick, Resourceful Commander." *America's Civil War* (September 1990): 12, 16 and 54.

Krick, Robert K. "The Confederate Pattons." In *The Shenandoah Valley Campaign of 1864.* Edited by Gary W. Gallagher. Chapel Hill: University of North Carolina Press, 2006.

Walls, R. Hal. "A History of the White Sulphur Rifles (Company G) and the Scouts and Guides (Company E) of Edgar's 26th Battalion of Patton's Brigade." *Journal of the Greenbrier Historical Society* 5, no. 3 (1989): 17–38.

Westnam, George S. "The Fourteenth Cavalry." *Pittsburgh Press*, October 8, 1961.

Books

Allardice, Bruce S. *Confederate Colonels: A Biographical Register*. Columbia: University of Missouri Press, 2008.

Anderson, Bart, ed. *The Sharples-Sharpless Family*. 3 vols. West Chester, PA: privately published, 1966.

Bates, Samuel P. *Martial Deeds of Pennsylvania*. Philadelphia: T.H. Davis & Co., 1876.

Baumgartner, Rick. *First Families of Huntington*. Huntington, WV: Huntington Publishing, 1977.

Cole, J.R. *History of Greenbrier County*. Lewisburg, WV: privately published, 1917.

Collins, Darrell L. *General William Averell's Salem Raid*. Shippensburg, PA: Burd Street Press, 1998.

———. *The Jones-Imboden Raid: The Confederate Attempt to Destroy the Baltimore & Ohio Railroad and Retake West Virginia*. Jefferson, NC: McFarland & Co., 2007.

Cozzens, Peter. *This Terrible Sound: The Battle of Chickamauga*. Urbana: University of Illinois Press, 1996.

Davis, William C., ed. *The Confederate General*. 6 vols. New York: National Historical Society, 1991.

Dickinson, Jack L. *8th Virginia Cavalry*. Lynchburg, VA: H.E. Howard, 1986.

———. *Wayne County, West Virginia in the Civil War*. Salem, MA: Higginson Books, 2003.

Emerson, Harrington. *Col. J.M. Schoonmaker and the Pittsburgh & Lake Erie Railroad: A Study of Personality and Ideals*. New York: Engineering Magazine, 1913.

Hardway, Ronald V. *On Our Own Soil: William Lowther Jackson and the Civil War in West Virginia's Mountains*. Charleston, WV: Quarrier Press, 2003.

Hayden, Horace Edwin. *Virginia Genealogies: A Genealogy of the Glassell Family of Scotland and Virginia*. Wilkes-Barre, PA: privately published, 1891.

Hunt, Roger D. *Colonels in Blue: Michigan, Ohio and West Virginia*. Jefferson, NC: McFarland Publishing, 2011.

———. *Colonels in Blue: Union Colonels of the Civil War, New York*. Atglen, PA: Schiffer Publishing, 2003.

Hunt, Roger D., and Jack R. Brown. *Brevet Brigadier Generals in Blue*. Gaithersburg, MD: Olde Soldier Books, 1990.

Kirshner, Ralph. *The Class of 1861: Custer, Ames, and Their Classmates After West Point*. Carbondale: Southern Illinois University Press, 1999.

Krick, Robert K. *Lee's Colonels: A Biographical Register of the Field Officers of the Army of Northern Virginia*. 4th ed. Dayton, OH: Morningside, 1992.

Lang, Theodore F. *Loyal West Virginia from 1861 to 1865*. Baltimore, MD: Deutch Publishers, 1895.

Levene, Ricardo. *A History of Argentina*. Chapell Hill: University of North Carolina Press, 1937.

Lowry, Terry. *Last Sleep: The Battle of Droop Mountain November 6, 1863*. Charleston, WV: Pictorial Histories Publishing Co., 1996.

———. *22nd Virginia Infantry*. Lynchburg, VA: H.E. Howard, 1988.

———. *26th Battalion Virginia Infantry*. Lynchburg, VA: H.E. Howard, 1991.

MacCorkle, William Alexander. *The White Sulphur Springs: The Traditions, History, and Social Life of the Greenbrier White Sulphur Springs*. New York: Neale Publishing Co., 1916.

McAulay, John D. *Carbines of the U.S. Cavalry 1861–1905*. Lincoln, RI: Andrew Mowbray, Inc., 1996.

McKinney, Tim. *The Civil War in Greenbrier County, West Virginia*. Charleston, WV: Quarrier Press, 2004.

Miller, Thomas Condit, and Hu Maxwell. *West Virginia and Its People*. 3 vols. New York: Lewis Historical Publishing Co., 1913.

Nelson, Robert H., and Emma L. Nelson. *James M. Corns: The Ancestry and Life of a Warrior*. Parker, CO: Outskirts Press, 2009.

Patton, Robert H. *The Pattons: A Personal History of an American Family*. New York: Crown Publishers, 1994.

Price, Andrew. "Plain Tales of Mountain Trails: The Midland Trail." In *West Virginia Blue Book*. Charleston, WV, 1928.

Reid, Whitelaw. *Ohio in the War: Her Statesmen, Generals, and Soldiers*. 2 vols. Cincinnati, OH: Robert Clarke Co., 1893.

Rhodes, Charles D. *History of the Cavalry of the Army of the Potomac, Including That of the Army of Virginia (Pope's), and also the History of the Operations of the Federal Cavalry in West Virginia During the War*. Kansas City, MO: Hudson-Kimberly, 1900.

Rice, Otis K. *A History of Greenbrier County*. Lewisburg, WV: Greenbrier Historical Society, 1986.

Rice, Otis K., and Stephen W. Brown. *West Virginia: A History*. 2nd ed. Lexington: University of Kentucky Press, 1993.

Scott, J.L. *45th Virginia Infantry*. Lynchburg, VA: H.E. Howard Co., 1989.

———. *Lowry's, Bryan's and Chapman's Batteries of Virginia Artillery*. Lynchburg, VA: H.E. Howard, 1988.

———. *36th and 37th Battalions Virginia Cavalry*. Lynchburg, VA: H.E. Howard, 1986.

Thomas, Dean S. *Round Ball to Rimfire: A History of Civil War Small Arms Ammunition*. 2 vols. Gettysburg, PA: Thomas Publications, 2002.

Warner, Ezra J. *Generals in Blue: Lives of the Union Commanders*. Baton Rouge: Louisiana State University Press, 1964.

———. *Generals in Gray: The Lives of the Confederate Commanders*. Baton Rouge: Louisiana State University Press, 1959.

Weaver, Jeffrey C. *The Virginia Home Guards*. Lynchburg, VA: H.E. Howard, 1996.

Wiley, Samuel T. *History of Monongalia County, West Virginia*. Kingwood, WV: Preston Publishing Co., 1883.

Williams, John Alexander. *West Virginia: A History*. New York: W.W. Norton & Co., 1984.

Wittenberg, Eric J. *The Union Cavalry Comes of Age: Hartwood Church to Brandy Station, 1863*. Dulles, VA: Brassey's, 2003.

Wong, J.W. *Deadly Dreams: Opium, Imperialism, and the Arrow War (1856–1860) in China*. Cambridge, UK: Cambridge University Press, 1998.

Woodworth, Steven E. *Six Armies in Tennessee: The Chickamauga and Chattanooga Campaigns*. Lincoln: University of Nebraska Press, 1998.

Index

I

J

K

L

M

S

T

U

V

W

Y

About the Author

Eric J. Wittenberg is an award-winning Civil War historian. Originally from southeastern Pennsylvania, he was educated at Dickinson College and the University of Pittsburgh School of Law. He is an attorney in private practice. He is also the author of more than fifteen published books on the Civil War and serves as a member of the Governor of Ohio's Commission on the Sesquicentennial of the Civil War and as vice-president of the Buffington Island Battlefield Preservation Foundation. He and his wife, Susan, and their two golden retrievers live in Columbus, Ohio.